LOST
CIRCUSES
OF OHIO

CONRADE C. HINDS

THE
History
PRESS

Published by The History Press
Charleston, SC
www.historypress.com

Cover images: Courtesy of the Fred Pfening Collection.

First published 2019

Manufactured in the United States

ISBN 9781467140690

Library of Congress Control Number: 2018963532

This book is dedicated to our grandchildren Audrey, Andromeda, Caleb and Lillian, and all the other grandchildren of my baby-boomer generation. If they can't attend a great circus show, then let them at least be able to read about it and experience the parades and excitement in their imagination.

CONTENTS

PREFACE

My love and interest in the circus began at age three when I started watching a television series called *Circus Boy* that aired from 1956 to 1958. It was about a twelve-year-old boy name Corky who was adopted by a circus and was a water boy to a baby elephant (he led the elephant to the water). The program shows Corky's participation and involvement in the behind-the-scenes life of the circus. The one thing that I appreciated most was a creed expressed by the talented and diverse circus cast that everyone should be accepted as he or she was born without judgement. That was profound to me because those were the initial years of the civil rights movement. The circus was a pleasant place for everyone and delighted the imagination as well.

This book is about a number of Ohio circuses, big and small, that are a living but forgotten part of our American heritage. I am of the opinion that most great things were invented in Ohio or by an Ohioan. And if neither case applies, then it was improved in Ohio. If that is narrow-minded thinking, then please forgive me, but first check the record. A lot of the modern entertainment world was developed in Ohio. Thomas Edison, who invented motion pictures, was from Ohio. Many of the lithograph billboard posters were printed in Cincinnati and Cleveland. And generations of movie stars, from Lillian Gish to Clark Gable and Dean Martin to Halle Berry, hail from Ohio.

The foundation for much of this entertainment industry started with the Ohio circuses that have been lost over the past century. First, the nineteenth-century circus yielded to vaudeville. Vaudeville yielded to radio and radio to talking motion pictures. Then along came the television and now computer games and iPads. Our culture gets lost because we are too involved with fads which are short-lived. So we lose a sense of self and our own culture.

The circus still lives even though Ringling is no more. And the lost circuses of Ohio can be found very easily by planting the images into the public's imagination. Today, you can use a computer or iPad to listen to calliope circus music. And since music is able to initiate and preserve emotions, you can close your eyes and be on the midway or in a circus parade down Main Street.

This book is also written as a salute to the Sells brothers (former Union soldiers during the Civil War), who were by all accounts ahead of their time in developing a working community known as Sellsville that was fully integrated by race and class.

ACKNOWLEDGEMENTS

T hank you to Tom Betti and Doreen Uhas Sauer for getting me started as an author of lost and forgotten history. Generous thanks to Fred D. Pfening III for his help in scholarly research, generous sharing of resources and constructive input.

Special thanks to Lenell Nussbaum and Peter Skartvedt, along with Josh and Eleanor Walters, for the use of the pleasant environments of their homes to get this project off the ground. My thanks to the Education Committee of the Columbus Landmarks Foundation for its encouragement and my grateful appreciation to John Sauer for his constructive editing. My gratitude to the many people who are no longer with us for their positive encouragement and how they opened the doors of opportunity for me over the past fifty-plus years.

Special thanks to my wife, Dr. Janet L. Hinds, and my late parents and grandparents—Dr. Conrade and Ada Hinds, and Russell and Ethel Davidson, respectively—for sharing their insight and wisdom. I'd also like to extend my warm acknowledgements to family and friends for their confidence in my ability and many thanks to John Rodrigue of The History Press. And my continued thanks to all those who supported preserving Ohio's great heritage of innovation.

OHIO'S CONTRIBUTION TO THE NINETEENTH-CENTURY GOLDEN AGE OF THE CIRCUS

Ohio has a strong heritage of being a state of many firsts and many innovations, such as the Wright brothers building the first powered flight airplane and Neil Armstrong being the first to set foot on the moon. The inventive spirit of the traditional Ohioan is rooted in an outstanding group of straightforward problem solvers. In the nineteenth century, Ohio was the American bottleneck, trapped between Canada and the provincial American South. As such, it was Ohio that captured and supplied the needs and wants of the East and West Coasts. It even supplied cities in the South by way of the Ohio and Mississippi Rivers to destinations like Louisville, St. Louis, Memphis and New Orleans.

The mid-nineteenth-century Civil War saw over 650,000 casualties and caused untold misery in the decades to follow. Many communities, especially in the South, had very little to look to for joy, peace and happiness because of the strong alienation that still existed between North and South, displaced relatives, families and the loss of a way of life that disenfranchised so many. Death was always a drink of water away from typhoid fever or dysentery and a host of other waterborne diseases. Also, in many parts of America, most people were still illiterate and lacked access to books or newspapers. There was not very much to really stir one's curiosity or spark a vivid imagination. And it was not uncommon for many people never to travel more than twenty to fifty miles from their place of birth in their entire lifetime.

All of this sets the stage for want and need in a wide range of communities throughout the country. The want was a chance to experience the world and all its profound wonders. The need was to safely have a venue where smiles could repeatedly be put on the faces of children and adults alike.

These needs and wants were filled by greats like James Bailey, Adam Forepaugh and many others. But there were three colossal circuses that served the need to spark and satisfy curiosity and paint a smile on the faces of a post–Civil War America. These circuses have been mostly forgotten over time primarily because they were acquired by the twentieth-century circus giant Ringling Bros. and Barnum & Bailey Circus.

In 2017, after 146 years of performing, the Ringling Bros. and Barnum & Bailey Circus announced its closing. The circus was billed as "The Greatest Show on Earth" and drew large crowds in the twentieth century. But interest in the iconic circus declined with the next century, due to high operating costs and long, costly legal battles with animal rights groups. The show's elephants were retired in May 2016. With the elimination of the elephant act, ticket sales began to decline more significantly. While there were and are today many compassionate animal trainers, historically, much of the animal cruelty was traditionally hidden behind closed doors. The nineteenth-century animal trainer Isaac Van Amburgh was renowned for his use of fear reinforcement. But we'll talk more about him in the first chapter.

Are circuses dying because they failed to evolve or are they declining because the audience has changed? The real answer is that the circus is still very much alive and with us. The traveling menageries have been replaced by municipal and private zoos and aquariums. World travel has been made comfortable and convenient for those desiring to participate and enjoy the discovery of new lands and cultures, not to mention how the pocket iPhone with internet service is able to connect you with people anywhere in the world. People are naturally curious creatures and other avenues are available to instantly satisfy that curiosity instead of having to wait for a show to come to a community once every year.

But for the average post–Civil War community, the expanded wonders of the world came to town or nearby several times a year. This was an event of great excitement to nearly everyone, young and old. Ohio was the winter headquarters for three of the large post–Civil War circuses. The state, of course, had a number of smaller circuses. But there were three major operations that proved to be extraordinary and served as the seeds for the next century of great showmen. The first was the multi-generation-owned John Robinson Circus that operated out of a Cincinnati suburb known as Terrace Park. Then there was in the capital city of Columbus, Ohio's very own Sells Brothers Circus. One local community fact that has been lost over the decades is that by 1890, the Sells & Barrett Circus was the third-largest circus in America, rivaled only by the Barnum and Bailey, and Adam Forepaugh Circuses. And in northern Ohio, there was the Walter L. Main Circus, operated by a young man barely out of his teens who proved to be a capable logistics manager working in cooperation with his father, William Main.

Lost Circuses of Ohio is a look at these and other nineteenth-century circus operations that paved the way for the modern twentieth-century American circus world.

CHAPTER 1

DEVELOPMENT OF THE AMERICAN CIRCUS

A variety of circus practices and elements can be dated throughout antiquity. Archeologists have uncovered Egyptian hieroglyphs that date as far back as 2500 B.C. that depict jugglers and acrobats. The ancient Roman circuses were greatly influenced by Egyptian and Greek spectacles. Many of these spectacles were re-created by the larger late nineteenth-century circuses in great detail. The fabulous exhibitions at the time of Christ included hand balancers, gymnasts, horse and chariot races, equestrian shows, staged battles, a wide variety of staged combat, and displays featuring trained wild animals. In Rome, the circus stadium consisted of tiers of seats in parallel rows with a horse track in the shape of a modern horseshoe. It is interesting to note that the Roman circus was one of the very few public events in which men and women were not seated in segregated sections.

After the fall of Rome, Europe lost the large animal-centered arenas. There were, however, in the Dark and Middle Ages, nomadic sideshows that performed at the various local town fairs throughout Europe. These performances featured animal trainers and skilled performers who traveled from town to town for a living. The European Gypsy people are thought to have ties between the ancient Romans and the circus that evolved out of the Renaissance era of Europe in the fourteenth and fifteenth centuries. The Gypsies maintained a wide variety of circus entertainment and skilled techniques for training animals.

The modern idea of a circus started during the late eighteenth-century industrial age and consisted of an elliptical or circular arena surrounded by parallel rows of bench seating. For the first time, showmen were combining various circus exhibitions to include acrobatic, equestrian, and other skilled performances. Beginning in London, Philip Astley (1742–1814) held the first performance of his show in 1768. One of Astley's key contributions to the circus was introducing skillful trick horse riding into a ring that he called the Circle. Later, to suit equestrian acts moving from one circus to another, the diameter of the circus ring was set at forty-two feet, which is the size ring needed for horses to circle comfortably at full gallop. Astley never referred to his show as a "circus." Instead that term was first used by his competitor John Hughes, who set up his Royal Circus in 1782 only a short distance from Astley's Amphitheatre of Equestrian Arts.

In England, circuses were often presented in buildings specifically designed for such large-scale entertainment. One such building was the London Hippodrome, which was erected as a multipurpose circus, menagerie, and variety theater facility where large wild animals such as lions and elephants appeared as part of a performance. Even in this era, there were realistic special effects executed, such as volcanic eruptions, floods, and even an occasional earthquake. Such displays proved to be real crowd-pleasers. The hippodrome originally was an ancient Grecian stadium for horse and chariot racing. The name is derived from the Greek words *hippos*, meaning "horse," and *dromos*, meaning "course."

John Bill Ricketts of Scotland (1769–1802) was a circus owner and skilled equestrian performer who brought the first model of a circus to the United States. He had a building constructed specifically for circus performances in Philadelphia in 1792 in which he conducted a riding school. After training a group of Pennsylvania horses and riders, he gave the first American multi-act circus performance on April 3, 1793. The show was called "Equestrian Exercises" and featured a series of exhibitions two or three times a week. President George Washington was in the audience during a performance at Ricketts's Circus in 1793. Ricketts had to contract for a building to be constructed in every town in which his show performed. In May 1794, Norfolk and Richmond, Virginia, were treated to their first circus performances by Ricketts. Ricketts and his company spent seven years introducing the circus to North America, venturing as far south as South Carolina and north into Quebec, Canada. But most of his travels focused on Virginia and the New England region, and his general headquarters was in Philadelphia.

There was not very much circus activity in America during the first decade of the nineteenth century. But the war from 1812 to 1815 with the British sparked a need for distraction and five circuses exhibited that year. As circus troupes began crossing the Allegheny Mountains, a westward movement began that took shows into the new American settlements in the Ohio and Mississippi River valleys. Communities such as Pittsburgh, Pennsylvania, and Cincinnati, Ohio, became major trading and manufacturing centers since British trade goods were now cut off. The Pepin and Breschard Circus, a French company renowned for giving quality performances, came to America in 1807. It played stands in Pittsburgh and Cincinnati in 1814 and played a season in 1815 in Lexington, Kentucky, and Chillicothe, Ohio.

Circus shows and menageries developed separately in America until the 1850s. In the early 1800s, a few circus shows were established around animal acts such as Isaac Van Amburgh and the Purdy, Welch & Co., greatly increasing the general popularity of the circus in America.

Isaac Van Amburgh (1808–1865) was an animal trainer of great fame and fortune. He possessed great physical strength and courage and performed with grace, firmness and self-possession. But he was also extremely cruel to animals and was known to frequently use a steel bar to beat his animals into submission. In many ways, we could safely state that he had absolutely no skill or talent for training animals. Van Amburgh would starve his lions for days prior to a performance until they were so weak from hunger that when it came time to perform he could easily force them into submission. With him, the style of animal acts changed from displays of docility to a demonstration of man's will over beast. The heritage of Van Amburgh could be regarded as the seed that undermined the Ringling circus in this new millennium. On a few occasions, however, Van Amburgh's animals would get an opportunity to sink their teeth into him and draw blood.

In later years, the July 25, 1863 *New York Clipper* reported that Van Amburgh & Company wintered in Dayton, Ohio, and was preparing for the following season through advanced advertising using billboards. The headliner elephant, Hannibal, was billed by a correspondent as having been very docile that winter, and so was his keeper, Frank Thomas, because he was recently married. The bills stated Hannibal's weight to be approximately fifteen thousand pounds, but he was a little less in weight since his tusks were removed. A Mr. Davis, who was an associate animal trainer, had a tussle with one of the tigers during the winter break and apparently Davis got the worst of it, because his arm was severely bitten in several places.

Menageries first played in Ohio in 1814, when the Museum of Living Animals exhibited a number of animals, including a tiger, an African ape, and a marmoset (a small species of primate native to South America). But the 1830s provided the first golden age of the traveling menageries. This was due in part to the anti-circus sentiments of many during this period because it was viewed as obscene and freakish. Conversely, the menagerie was viewed as an educational and enlightening family experience. Showmen would even quote Biblical verses associated with animals in the advertisements to illustrate man's dominion over beasts. These early menageries were viewed by nineteenth-century Americans as collections of exotic creatures of nature. They included camels, lions, polar bears, sea lions and large tropical snakes to name a few.

Circus owner Joshuah Purdy Brown (1802–1834) initiated the use of extra-large canvas tents for the circus performances. He toured his circus with a combined menagerie for the first time. In 1825, he partnered with Lewis Bailey in a circus venture that was his first season under canvas and the beginning of the use of tents for traveling circuses. Circus historian Stuart Thayer credits him with Americanizing the circus and initiating the wagon-traveling caravan show complete with its own portable theater to make one-day stands in various towns possible. Thayer also makes an excellent point that since Brown had his show on the road as early as 1825, he must have been a competent manager with good judgment and shrewd sense of business to survive the difficulties and hardships of pioneer travel and competition.

The canvas tent big top was a commonplace sight at circuses by the mid-1830s. This versatile mobility allowed the circus owner to plan a show-route season in one hundred or more different communities, large and small. Performances could be given five to six days per week, but this introduced a logistical nightmare that generally was not an issue with a performance in a building in one place. These circuses now required wagons and horses to transport supplies and equipment and needed experienced personnel to drive the wagons and erect the tents. The use of large big top tents meant a significant increase in daily expenses and altered the working relationship between the owners and their employees. Previously, the owner either rented or built a costly arena. But now owners had to bear the cost of wagons, horses and teamsters to transport the show on wheels. The performers and musicians were now constantly with the show, and a reliable income flow was required to offset the constant daily expense of providing food and some type of berths for sleeping.

Greater mobility meant that circuses could travel more frequently and play more stands, but it also meant that owners had far less time to build up the audience interest in the show, which meant increased revenue. This called for strategic advertising, and that meant good business for local newspapers that were pleased to carry larger illustrated ads. Plus, there was a growing need to usher the audiences into their seats quickly and efficiently. The American circus slowly evolved before the Civil War. But during the postwar era, we see the first two-ring circus tent appearing in 1873. As the tents increased in size, the performers were naturally more removed from the general spectators. This ushered in a circus golden era that meant the acts needed to be more exciting and breathtaking. These criteria only increased transportation logistics and general cost.

As stated, the early American circuses were transported from town to town by horse-drawn wagons and also riverboats. Canalboats followed with the opening of the Ohio-Erie Canal to commercial traffic. These methods were not cost-effective and not always reliable given the conditions of plain dirt roads and water transportation due to seasonal weather. A common itinerary of show stands followed the communities along the National Road that started at Cumberland, Maryland, to Wheeling, West Virginia, and on to Columbus, Ohio, by 1833. The 1830s and 1840s saw both circuses and menageries spread their regional influence to a larger part of the country. With new transportation infrastructure such as the opening of new canals and the building of roads, the circus was quick to make use of advancements.

But with the introduction of rail travel, a circus could log up to a hundred miles in a single night at twenty-five to thirty miles per hour. Railroad transport for circuses began in Ohio in the late 1850s on the short line railways. However, the big shows took to the rails in 1872 when P.T. Barnum and W.C. Coup put their East Coast show on rails. This allowed the circus to play towns in the Midwest and beyond. In some cases, it also expanded the season by being able to get to warmer locations in the South during autumn months. This created the model of the "railroad circus" that would define the circus industry through the next century. No longer did the circus have to depend on wagon caravans to convey large quantities of materials and labor from town to town. Once rail transportation became an option, many shows switched over to this form of conveyance in a single season. An entire circus show could travel from its winter quarters to virtually any place in the country that was serviced by a railroad. And in many cases, special excursion trains were established to bring people from outlying areas to see the show. This helped to increase audience attendance by drawing in people who otherwise could not get to the show.

Another circus pioneer was Dan Rice (1823–1900), a multitalented showman who presented himself most famously as a clown and was preeminent before the Civil War. Born Daniel McLaren in New York City,

Rice (he preferred his mother's maiden name) gained nineteenth-century fame with many talents, most of which involved performing as a clown figure in various circuses. In addition to his comic talents, Rice was an animal trainer, songwriter, commentator, political humorist, strong man, actor, director, producer, dancer and even a political figure. He ran for the U.S. Senate, the House of Representatives and president of the United States. But lacking any real political experience, he withdrew from each of the campaigns.

At the height of his career, Rice's clown character was easily recognizable and renowned. Dan Rice was an innovator who coined the terms "one-horse show" and "greatest show." He was a leading personality in the new nineteenth-century American "pop culture" brought on by the technological changes of the Industrial Revolution. Many regard Rice as the modern model for the Uncle Sam patriotic symbol, while others argue that Samuel Wilson, a meatpacker from Troy, New York, who supplied rations for American troops during the War of 1812, was the original influence. Either way, it appears that historically both men were willing to render their services to their country.

Rice started his career as an entertainer around 1836 and got his first big break in 1841, when he got a job presenting a pig named Sybil who could do many tricks, including the ability to tell time. From there, he moved on to singing and dancing. He leveraged his popularity and changed his presentation style by starring in various parodies of works by William Shakespeare, including that of *Dan Rice's Version of Othello* and *Dan Rice's Multifarious Account of Shakespeare's Hamlet*. He would perform these with various songs and dialects. Rice was known as an innovative clown because he would mingle jokes, solemn thoughts, civic observations and songs into his performances. He was the prototype for today's standup comedians.

The advancements in circus venues and popular culture in post–Civil War America and his legendary talents under the big top have mostly been forgotten. But toward the end of his career, Rice could still garner a crowd and that is why he was under contract with John Robinson as late as 1882. Dan Rice died in 1900.

By the 1840s, many of the large circuses were wintering in Ohio for multiple seasons in the bigger cities. A wide range of shows played Columbus in 1846, including Raymond & Waring, S.P. Stickney's New Orleans, Welch, Mann and Delavan, and Rockwell & Stone. Zanesville developed into a western headquarters for James Raymond, who wintered his menagerie in an old foundry from the 1840s to the 1850s. Cincinnati developed into a major circus center by the late 1850s and had both circuses and menageries in winter residence. Van Amburgh's Menagerie wintered there because of the site's proximity to the Ohio River. The barge for Spalding & Rogers Floating Palace was constructed in Cincinnati in 1852, and the show played various communities along the Ohio-Mississippi river system.

American showman Phineas Taylor Barnum (1810–1891) was also a politician and businessman who was renowned for promoting celebrated hoaxes. He first made a name for himself in 1835 by selling tickets to see an elderly female slave name Joyce Heth. Barnum claimed (as he was also told) that she was 161 years old and had been President George Washington's nursemaid. Shortly after she began a solo exhibition for Barnum, Heth died in February 1836. Award-winning author Harriet A. Washington's book *Medical Apartheid* states that Barnum then sold tickets to her autopsy, which was performed by a surgeon in front of some 1,500 spectators. The surgeon concluded that Heth was no more than 80 years old. It was Heth's show appearances that propelled Barnum to fame, and he was appointed treasurer of the Aaron Turner Circus.

For most of his public career, P.T. Barnum was a museum owner, but his name still carries a very strong association with the circus. In 1841, he initially operated Barnum's American Museum in New York City, in the former Scudder's American Museum building. Barnum made a point of expanding the existing exhibits and introduced a freak show of various oddities along with a variety of exotic animals to give the experience of a zoo-like menagerie. Using Barnum's name as a draw for an audience, his partners took the museum on tours as a road show in 1849 as "P.T. Barnum's Grand Traveling American Museum."

Barnum was never the sole owner of a big top circus. He worked with a number of business partners and produced some of the most popular circus spectacles of the late nineteenth century. Two of his early partners were Seth B. Howes of the Barnum Caravan Circus (circa 1851–54) and Hyatt Frost of Barnum and Van Amburgh (circa 1865–67).

Along with a number of investment setbacks, Barnum's museum burned to the ground twice. The first fire was in July 1865, and although Barnum attempted to re-establish the museum at another location in New York, it also caught fire and was completely destroyed in 1868. Following this disaster, he went into a self-imposed retirement and began writing his autobiography.

In late 1870, circus entrepreneurs William Cameron Coup (1836–1895) and Dan Castello (1834–1909) jointly urged Barnum out of retirement, and the three men established P.T. Barnum's Museum, Menagerie and Circus.

James A. Bailey, businessman and circus entrepreneur. Circa 1880. *Library of Congress.*

The circus that evolved into the P.T. Barnum show had previously been titled the Dan Castello Great Show & Egyptian Caravan of 1870, which toured the Great Lakes on board the propeller-driven steamer *Benton* during that season. Castello, Coup and P.T. Barnum each put up equal amounts of money to take the Barnum show out from 1871 to 1875. This enterprise was a full-scale traveling variety show in which the "museum" was an exhibition of animal and human oddities.

The first documented transport of an American circus by rail was in 1838, when Charles Bacon and Edward Derious moved parts of their show in Georgia. There were a few minor attempts to move shows in the following decade, but it was not until the early 1850s that circus owners seriously began considering transporting their shows via railroad. It is known that in 1851, the Stone & Madigan Circus used the railroad to transport its show. In 1853, the Railroad Circus & Crystal Amphitheatre became the first show to tour for an entire season by rails, and in 1855 the Great Western Railroad Circus followed suit. Beginning in 1856, Gilbert R. Spalding and Charles J. Rogers opened the season with the Spalding & Rogers Railroad Circus, using nine custom-built railcars. The season tour started in Washington, D.C., and traveled through the states of Pennsylvania, New York, Massachusetts, Maine, Michigan and Ohio, as well as the British provinces. In Ohio, it continued its tour along the Ohio River aboard the Spalding and Rogers Floating Palace.

Another nineteenth-century circus great was James Anthony Bailey (1845–1906), who was originally born James Anthony McGinnis. He was orphaned at the age of eight and was employed as a bellhop in Pontiac, Michigan. McGinnis was a teenager when he was discovered by Frederic Harrison Bailey, who was a nephew of American circus pioneer Hachaliah Bailey. F.H. Bailey gave young McGinnis a job as his personal assistant, and the two traveled together for many years. Given the degree of trust and the nature of guidance McGinnis received, he decided to adopt Frederic H. Bailey's surname and became known as James A. Bailey for the balance of his life.

CHAPTER 2

THE JOHN ROBINSON CIRCUS

Old" John F. Robinson was the founder and longtime owner of the John Robinson Circus and one of the great innovators in American circus history. The patriarch of the Robinson family was born on July 6, 1804, at Little Falls, New York, and died on August 4, 1888. In his younger days, he gained an enviable reputation as an equestrian. After leaving home, he started working as a hostler with the Captain Page Menagerie and the Parsons & McCracken Circus, where he became a performer. In the years that followed, he was with Aron Turner's Circus, Stewart's Amphitheater, Hawkin's Circus, Benedict and Haddoch Circus and the Zoological Institute. At age fifteen, he was employed as a watchman near Boston at the winter headquarters of Henry Rockwell and while there practiced riding horses at night. His name first appears in a billing advertisement for the Boston Circus that was playing a stand in Columbus, Ohio, on November 24, 1832. In this program printed in the *Ohio State Journal*, John Robinson's name appears as a stilt dancer. By the time he was eighteen, he was a four-horse rider with the circus owned by Matthew Buckley and Chauncey Weeks. He stayed with the show until it was sold at auction in Somers, New York, in August 1837. Charles H. Bacon formed a new circus in Baltimore in November 1837 and hired Robinson, who remained with it and the successor show, Bacon & Derious, until late 1838. (It should be stated that these statements are difficult to confirm as they represent nearly two centuries of hearsay, unconfirmed newspaper accounts and memory recollection.)

Old John F. Robinson, founder of the original Robinson Circus. Circa 1890. Russell-Morgan Lithograph. *Cincinnati & Hamilton County Library.*

For a long time, there was a "myth" that the John Robinson show was first established in 1824. This was thought to have been for publicity's sake and the bragging rights of being the oldest established show in America. But thanks to the research of Richard E. Conover, we are able to conclude that the Robinson Circus was founded in 1842. This is because a newspaper article from a January 1870 *Cincinnati Chronicle* details a close call that Old John Robinson had on New Year's Eve 1841 when a rampage by an elephant called Columbus occurred just outside New Orleans. James Raymond's circus and Noel Waring's menagerie had been showing separately in Louisiana but decided to rendezvous three miles north of Algiers, Louisiana. The strategy was for the combined show, which was the largest that has ever appeared in the South in the nineteenth century, to march into the Crescent City on New Year's Day.

In 1846, the two men established the Robinson & Eldred Combination Circus. Their show was playing a stand in Covington, Kentucky, in 1850, when Old John developed a severe eye ailment that required special attention. He was referred to a physician who was an eye specialist just across the Ohio River in Cincinnati. By 1850 standards, Cincinnati was one of the most cosmopolitan cities in the Midwest, and this suited Old John just fine in light of his growing reputation. Cincinnati was a major transportation trading center with access to the Deep South via the Ohio and Mississippi Rivers. In 1852, Robinson decided to re-establish his home and headquarters in Cincinnati, where he raised his family—John Jr., Gil, Frank, James, Charles and a daughter Katie. Katie married Robert Stickney Sr. and shortly died in childbirth. All of his children were from his second marriage. His first, to Margaret Yates in Schenectady, New York, in 1835, ended in divorce. He then married Elizabeth Bloomer, who was an equestrienne. She died on Christmas Eve in 1879.

Gradually, Robinson began transferring the running of the John Robinson show to his sons. He purchased a home at Seventh and College Streets in

Cincinnati in 1854, and in 1856, Old John Robinson retired. But his love of the circus business proved too great. So in 1857, he bought out the entire Flagg and Aymar Circus and renamed the outfit the Robinson Show. During the season of 1858, "Bill" Lake, the clown, and Robinson formed a partnership that lasted until 1862. During this time, he made an alliance with his brother Alexander for two seasons.

In 1860, the Robinsons bought land in what later became Terrace Park, Ohio. There, they built a seventeen-room Italianate brick mansion, along with a practice ring and barns for the circus animals as winter headquarters.

His eldest son, John F. Robinson Jr. (1843–1921), assumed management of the John Robinson Circus with his brothers in 1871, after their father retired the second time. John F. Jr. was initially trained as a bareback rider, tumbler and leaper. He eventually had to quit performing in the ring because of weight gain. He had six children with his first wife, who died August 6, 1889. Of the six children, only four survived her: John G., Caroline, Pearl and Cad.

Gilbert N. Robinson (1845–1928) was the second son of Old John Robinson and began as a tumbler and carpet acrobat, making his ring debut in 1848, at age three, with the Robinson and Eldred show. When his brothers took over the management of the John Robinson Circus in the spring of 1871, Gilbert served as both general advance agent and treasurer. On November 16, 1875, he married circus rider Emma Lake Thatcher of Memphis, Tennessee. Gilbert died in Cincinnati at eighty-four years of age.

Third son James H. Robinson served as the front door superintendent and assistant manager, but at the tender age of thirty-three, he died in September 1880 while traveling in advance of the show.

Frank M. Robinson (1849–1882) was the fourth son of Old John Robinson and was a very accomplished rider and clown with his father's show and others for many years. He became treasurer in 1879 and part owner of the John Robinson show. On July 14, 1879, Frank married Frankie Bailey. He was only thirty-two years old when he died in Cincinnati.

Charles C. Robinson was the youngest son of "Old" John Robinson and was not active in the performance ring. However, he was the general assistant and later treasurer of the operation.

Until the beginning of 1871, "Old" John had been the sole proprietor of the Old John Robinson show for the previous nine years. Over the years, he had amassed a sizable amount of wealth and property. In 1875, he became the Republican Party's nominee for the mayor of Cincinnati and was only narrowly defeated. At the time of his death in Cincinnati, on August 4, 1888,

Right: John F. Robinson sitting atop Tillie the elephant. Circa 1905. *Cincinnati & Hamilton County Library.*

Below: Robinson Circus advance rail coach no. 1 with staff was used to promote the circus with billboard signs and news articles ahead of the show's arrival. Circa 1905. *University of Kentucky Library Archive.*

The official John Robinson Circus letterhead. 1892. *Cincinnati & Hamilton County Library.*

his estate was valued at over $1 million. One biographer, in commenting upon the character of the man, stated that Robinson was a diamond in the rough but his heart was always in the right place and the memory of the pioneer circus showman will long be fondly cherished.

The early 1890s were a challenge for the Robinson show, and in 1895, the show didn't go out on tour. Then the "Old" John Robinson Circus went under new management for 1896–97, when John F. Jr. collaborated with Charles and William E. Franklin to form the John Robinson & Franklin Brothers Enormous Show Combined. The menagerie of the Robert Hunting show was acquired and added to the already sizeable one of the combined circuses. The Ringlings stepped up to provide financial assistance and some equipment to the Robinsons for the 1898 season. By 1899, the Robinson family was able to regain full control of the show.

The eldest son of John F. Jr., John G. (Papa) Robinson (1872–1935) was born in Cincinnati and engaged in show business all of his life. He was a circus rider at age eighteen and at twenty became assistant manager of the John Robinson Circus. In 1909, John F. Jr. sold the circus to John G. for $100,000 under the table. This action apparently cured an estrangement between the father and son that was caused by John F. Jr.'s marriage to his nurse, Mary Maud Logan. The ceremony took place in Clarksville, Tennessee, on September 22, 1908, in a private rail coach belonging to the Robinson Circus. After filing in a Cincinnati court to put an end to all legal action, John F. Jr. gave John G. a bill of sale for $1.00 and other considerations. This conveyed all of the circus property known as John

A Chillicothe, Ohio street parade of the joint Robinson Franklin Circus. 1896. *Chillicothe and Ross County Public Library.*

Robinson Ten Big Shows to John G. and terminated a nasty legal process. But John F. Jr. retained a life-long interest in the property that would net him at least $10,000 ($277,000 in 2018 dollars) a year. This put an end to the father and son estrangement during the 1908 tenting season.

A few years later in a Cincinnati court, John F. Jr. lost a legal battle with both of his daughters. The judgment stated that he must turn over to Pearl R. Lamkin and Caroline R. Stevens all the stock that he had been holding and that was left to them by their deceased mother. In addition, the court also required that he forfeit $30,000 in accrued dividends, the stocks being valued at nearly $270,000 ($7 million in 2018 dollars).

As a result, on October 26, 1912, in Cincinnati, Robinson declared bankruptcy for the second time in thirty days. But John F. Jr. claimed he was solvent and able to pay his debts if given time. In an appeal, he won a $320,000 ($8 million in 2018 dollars) suit against his two daughters from the Ohio Supreme Court, in Columbus, on June 24, 1913. At age thirty-eight, his daughter Pearl died of influenza at her home in Chicago, during the horrific 1918 influenza pandemic.

Her older brother John G. continued until 1912, when he did not take the show on the road because of financial reservations stirred by the presidential

Robinson Circus admission ticket wagon was generally the first stop for most patrons. Circa 1892. *Ohio History Connection.*

election year. So he split the circus into individual vaudeville acts and toured under the auspices of the Western Vaudeville Association. He then sold the title rights and remaining equipment of the John Robinson Ten Big Shows to Jerry Mugivan and Bert Bowers (spring 1916), and it later passed into the hands of John Ringling, the only living brother in 1929 when the John Robinson show was acquired with the rest of the American Circus Corporation.

The John Robinson Military Elephant act appeared for several years at indoor circuses, parks, fairs and at special performances and eventually came under the management of son John IV (1893–1954). John G. Robinson served as a director of the Cincinnati Zoo, and secretary and director of the U.S. Playing Card Company. At the age of sixty-three, he passed away at his home, 3010 Reading Road, Cincinnati, Ohio.

During the tenure of the various generations of the Robinson Circus management, a wide variety of events, triumphs, conundrums and assorted mishaps occurred. Here are a few historic highlights.

Circuses were reviewed by the press in the same manner as a Broadway play, and often the reviewer was too far left or right depending on personal preferences. An example of this is that one reviewer in Wood River, Idaho, in 1875 regarded the Robinson show to be superior to W.W. Cole's circus in some areas, and desperately inferior in others. But the reviewer admitted that Robinson had the best record of any show on the road. He continued by stating that "the circus is all anyone cares to speak about on circus day and everyone who had seen W.W. Cole's circus would naturally make a comparison and that any comparisons would not favor John Robinson's Ten Shows Consolidated." The reporter then proceeded to itemize the various deficiencies by starting on the size of the elephant, which was not as large as Cole's pachyderm by two feet, although Old Mary of Robinson's was questionably billed as the oldest known of the species. "Cole had a whole drove of camels; Robinson had none. Cole's procession was much longer than Robinson's parade. Cole's procession included a first-class calliope and a new steam pipe organ, numerous cavalcades of riders, couriers, Shetland ponies and a large number of thoroughbred horses. Robinson's lacked the cavalcade, the Shetlands, the thoroughbreds and they evidently fell far behind Cole in the number of employees." The reviewer could not understand how John Robinson's reputation as a circus showman was superior to Cole's. The employees admitted that only half the show was driven through Hailey, Idaho, and that only half the big tent was brought to Wood River, Idaho.

A team of camels pulling a wagon as part of a Robinson Circus street parade. Circa 1909. *University of Kentucky Library Archive.*

"If half the tent was left behind, so must a good part of the show also. The tent, as erected, would accommodate 5000 to 6000 spectators, while the big canvas, when spread to its full limit, has a capacity of considerably more patrons. In Denver, previous, the Robinson circus gave three performances, which were attended by extremely large crowds. At the side shows the change is promptly and correctly made and patrons do not have the life tortured out of them by gaming swindlers." The reviewer further stated that "the show was worth the price of admission, even though the entire John Robinson great circus wasn't on site" and that there were only two small rings, with a double stage between. "The reason for this (instead of there being but one large ring) is that both human performers and horses alike are trained to go in a curve of forty-two feet, to rise, fall vault, dance, etc., at a certain angle. Plus, if the curve was increased, it would be impossible for the performers to maintain their equilibrium. This is why the circus rings are all the same size."

Circuses in the nineteenth century would often encounter an unruly patron who had too much to drink or just a bad day. But in 1873, the Robinson circus played a stand in Jacksonville, Texas, that resulted in a small riot, gunfights, stabbings and an intense escape. Circus day brought every sort of person to town for the event. The greater the crowd, the better the proceeds were at the gate for the circus, sideshow and gaming. As expected, men would get drunk, and unruly and small disputes would escalate into a fight between locals and the show staff. Such fights would take place regularly, with combatants using fists, clubs, guns and knives. However, the show staff was trained and equipped to handle these brawls.

Robinson Circus Street Parade down Third Street in Dayton, Ohio. Boston Store pictured across the street later became part of the Elder-Beerman chain of stores that finally closed in 2018. Circa 1897. *Dayton Public Library.*

Robinson's No. 2 Calliope echoed a delightful sound that could be heard throughout any community. Circa 1893. *Peru Indiana Public Library.*

The Jacksonville riot started when several local rowdies looking for a fight interfered with bringing horses into the ring for a show. So two staff members, one name DeVere, with the help of another promptly removed the rowdies from the ring by taking them by the throat and shoulders and ushering them out. There were many in the audience who witnessed this action and sided against the circus for harming a local citizen. In fact, they wanted to kill DeVere. Jacksonville had a lot of bars where the rowdies began getting drunk and mad enough for the spark of revenge to translate into action.

The locals went to the circus train with a warrant to arrest DeVere. Gil Robinson had DeVere hidden in the woods down in a patch of brush. With loaded rifles and shotguns, the circus staff was prepared for trouble. In the meantime, the circus was loading to move out for the next stand when shots were fired. The circus continued to get ready to pull out while also holding off the locals. Upon the circus's moving out, the townspeople had planned to sabotage a small bridge crossing, but that plan failed. The townsfolk of course told a different story. As word spread of this event, needless to

Robinson Circus labor and lot staging staff were often only hired locally part-time; this was a common circus business practice. Circa 1897. *Cincinnati & Hamilton County Library.*

say it would be a number of years before another circus would dare play Jacksonville, Texas.

Old John Robinson was well known by his associates for being blunt and to the point, quick tempered and eloquent in his use of profanity. But in contrast, he was also a man with a strong inclination to be charitable toward children. On November 19, 1875, a Tennessee newspaper, the *Memphis Daily Appeal*, gave an account of Old John's charity with a headline that read:

> *Hundred Orphans Had a Benefit at Old John Robinson's Circus and Menagerie Yesterday Afternoon.*

> *Yesterday and last night thousands of people both old and young attended John Robinson's Great Circus and Menagerie show. Last night there was a very large attendance and a most brilliant performance. John Lowlow, the clown, seemed to be inspired by the joy of the crowd, and kept the people almost continually laughing. Such entertainment is not often witnessed at a circus. The audience was composed of the representatives of the elite of the city, a compliment all the more noticeable when it is known that the Memphis theater, with the "Two Orphans" was also crowded. Old John*

Robinson, in accordance with his time honored custom invited the orphans of Memphis to attend his big show. Such generosity will be appreciated and gratefully remembered by our people who long since have learned to esteem John Robinson for his many excellent qualities, and to value the worth of the magnificent show in which he offers the public. The present show is superior to any he has yet given. Every feature of the show will not fail to excite interest and pleasure. The equestrians are unsurpassed in grace, dexterity and precision. The trained dogs, tight-rope performances, trapeze acts and acrobatics are brilliant, graceful and fearless. Every feature of this show is of such an order as to satisfy public expectation. It is second to none in the country, and far surpasses the generality of shows that visit the south. It is a show which owes credit to the genius of John Robinson, and gives him additional claim to the reputation accorded him of being the best, most popular and clever showman in America. His menagerie is perhaps the most varied in its character and excellent in its collections that Memphis has ever seen. The old as well as the young, the scholar and the student, will each find in Old John Robinson's menagerie an instructive pleasure. Old John Robinson goes from here to Hernando, Sardis, Grenada, and elsewhere in Mississippi. The citizens of our sister State will be afforded an entertainment of unbounded merit, and should not fail to pay Old John a call. He took his departure this morning via the Mississippi and Tennessee railroad for Hernando, where he exhibits today and tonight.

The children of the Church Home Orphan Asylum yesterday attended the show, under the charge of Miss Nancy Scott and Mrs. W. S. Pickett, Superintendent of the asylum. Due to the disagreeable weather the attendance yesterday was not very large, and although the net proceeds amounted to only eighty-one dollars, Old John Robinson with characteristic generosity donated one hundred dollars [$2,300 in today's dollars] *to the orphans. The show is excellent in every respect, and during its three-day performance in Memphis it afforded unbounded joy, pleasure and laughter to thousands of people.*

The week previous to the circus coming to Memphis, the six members of the city council voted on a petition presented to the mayor, asking him to remit the tax on John Robinson's circus for the performance on November 18 because of the benefit to the orphans. The tax was ordered remitted. The Memphis newspaper the following day also printed a card which fully explained the joyful results of the Old John Robinson benefit show for the Church Orphans Home:

> *To: Messrs. John Robinson and Sons:*
> *Gentlemen, on behalf of the orphans of Church Orphans Home, allow me to thank you for your liberal donation, amounting to one hundred dollars. I sincerely regret that your engagements while in our city prevented you from visiting the Orphans home, which you have supported and so generously contributed to during your visit and former occasions. The children will long remember their fine afternoon of entertainment and fully appreciate the warm clothing your charity has provided them with for the approaching winter.*
>
> *Wishing you much success that must attend such benevolence, I am very sincerely yours,*
> *Mrs. W.S. Pickett, Superintendent of the Church Orphans Home*

The initial public joy of experiencing the circus normally began with a parade down the community's main street. The 1893 John Robinson Circus Parade began with John Robinson III and his $3,000 tandem of Arabian horses. He was followed by the big bandwagon drawn by eight black horses, with Henry Becker and band with singers positioned up top. Next were eight English carriages occupied by women performers and miniature cages drawn by Shetland ponies. Four camels were drawing four open-cage wagons. The first contained African pelicans; the second had wild Russian bears; the third wagon had a polar bear with the Continental drum corps seated up top. And the fourth open-cage wagon carried a Black Sea bear. These were followed by a tableau cart with a clown band and another open-cage wagon of warthogs. The animal procession included a herd of elephants, water buffaloes and sacred cattle and a carved Roman lion's den with the star lion Sultan and his family inside. This was followed by the Queen Ann chariot–cage wagon that carried a large group of Bengal tigers inside and a mirror-cage wagon carrying leopards, which was a treat of excitement to the young onlookers. Another tableau wagon with African antelopes followed, along with a very ornate bandwagon that was drawn by sixteen horses. There was a cage wagon with a wide variety of different species of monkeys inside, a chariot–cage wagon with a pair of "horned horses" inside, and a cage wagon with ostriches and kangaroos. And bringing up the rear was a blaring and sensational steam calliope that was drawn by twenty-four Shetland ponies.

Robinson Circus parade Leopard Wagon with tableau sides removed. Circa 1907. *University of Kentucky Library Archive.*

Robinson Circus menagerie animals carefully being unloaded from a company-owned boxcar. Circa 1890. *Cincinnati & Hamilton County Library.*

After the parade, the public would line up at the ticket booth to gain admission to the big top. Probably one of the most ambitious circus presentations of 1891 was a venture requiring a sizable investment on behalf of the John Robinson Circus. It was a magnificent production on a scale of opulent splendor never before seen regarding the biblical spectacle of Solomon, his temple and the Queen of Sheba. The performance was a spectacle, with grand scenic effects, impressive in pomp and pageantry, and realistic in its reproduction of the patriarchal era. The show was also sacred in holding to its biblical associations and the ballet of the entrances, overall groupings and poses. The show starts with the visit of the Queen of Sheba to King Solomon's court with her immense and richly costumed entourage of attendants, the Judgment of Solomon, the Sacrificial Ceremonies of the Temple and presentation of Solomon's seven hundred wives. It continued with a grand processional pageant to meet the beautiful queen, the walls and City of Jerusalem, the inner court of Solomon's Temple and the great Throne of Ivory. The audience was also treated to seeing a replica of the Ark of the Covenant, the dazzling ballet of lovely Cresset girls and a myriad of feature details that were withheld from the public and pre-show press descriptions.

On August 28, 1894, the (Xenia) *Ohio Republican* newspaper stated that the John Robinson production "Solomon and Queen of Sheba" was so grand that a new art form had been established as an aid for presenting biblical lore. The Robinson circus retained the services of Cincinnati native John Rettig, who devoted over a year to personal research in Palestine, Jerusalem and the Holy Land. This allowed him to skillfully reproduce the notable scenes, incidents and events that occurred during the regal administration of the great Hebrew patriarch and king. The talented Rettig coordinated and designed other productions, including one for the Ringling circus.

In addition to the glamour of the Solomon performance, the John Robinson Big Show featured a death-defying act by Mephisto, who was billed as the wonder of the age, in his awe-inspiring, unparalleled act of circling the loop in an automobile. In 1894, this was truly a sensation and without precedent for spectators to see such a feat using a horseless carriage.

The final curtain call for the original John Robinson Ten Big Shows came in 1911. The John Robinson family of Cincinnati (Terrace Park), Ohio, represented three nineteenth-century generations of successful circus management. "Old" John Robinson, the founder, passed on in late 1888 and left his legacy to his son John F. Jr. and grandson John G., to carry on and flourish even further.

Left: Unidentified female cast member in the role of the Queen of Sheba for the Robinson Circus. Circa 1895. *Cincinnati & Hamilton County Library*.

Below: King Solomon and the Queen of Sheba Show cast lineup. Circa 1895. *Cincinnati & Hamilton County Library*.

The 1911 season opened at the Cincinnati Armory on April 18 and played for a week. The first stand under canvas was in Wilmington, Ohio. The full traveling circus required forty-seven railcars. The immense spread of canvas and the many cages, dens and parade wagons were of such an elaborate design and glittering in new paint that they presented a sight one would not soon forget. Rudolph Gessely was treasurer and ticket seller, and the press agent was a man called Punch Wheeler. Colonel Cal Towers was the manager of the "Big Double Museum and Wonders of Creation," better known as a "Giant Galaxy of Creations Climax Marvels" or sideshow. Bill Davis served as lot superintendent, and Edward Van Skaik was the big show announcer and official mailman. Charles Gerlach was bandmaster of the big show band, while Alex Berry was head leader of the sideshow band and minstrels, and Buggy Stump was an official trainmaster.

The 1911 season big top featured six center poles, three rings and one elevated stage, and the menagerie tent had eight poles. William DeMott was the equestrian director and a bareback rider, and he did a four-horse jockey act and worked with the equestrienne Eunice DeMott. The DeComa Troupe was a four-person big aerial trapeze act. There were three other troupes of acrobats, which included the DeBoliens, the Linnigers and the

Here, seated, is the Robinson Circus band in full uniform. Circa 1898. *University of Cincinnati Library Archive.*

Robinson Circus featured a Civil War–era ironclad ship float in its street parades. Circa 1900. *Cincinnati & Hamilton County Library.*

Waltons from Toledo, Ohio, who also did a Roman statuary act. Warren Travis was billed as the world's strongest man. He could lift fourteen men on a platform, support a bridge walkway over which horses passed, shoulder immense dumbbells and bend bars of iron with his bare hands. In one performance, Travis allowed an auto to be driven over him containing four people. Berry and Hicks appeared in novelty balancing and breakaway ladder displays. Also in the lineup were the Howards, a troupe of four performers on unsupported ladders appearing on an elevated stage. The O'Wessneys presented their English carrying act and trained horse displays, while Captain Alber's eight trained polar bears and Millie Marguerite with trained lions appeared as separate acts in the steel arena. A few of the clowns were Newport and Stirk, Bill Ashe, the Downing Brothers, McCammon and Robettas, and John Mangels, the club juggler.

The big top show closed with Prince Lucci and six Russian Cossacks performing daring and breakneck riding displays. A troupe of Sioux gave their war dances and remembrances of the Old West, concluding with the hanging of the horse thief.

A bad windstorm struck the show July 4 in Union City, Pennsylvania, at noon. Both the matinee and evening shows were given with just the sidewall enclosure in place minus the top, but the crowd was sizable. At Ogdensburg, New York, another storm was encountered, blowing down the cookhouse

Robinson Circus clowns and comic performers. Circa 1899. *Cincinnati & Hamilton County Library.*

Robinson Circus Wild West street parade. Circa 1899. *Cincinnati & Hamilton County Library.*

just prior to supper. At Bellefontaine, Ohio, after a downpour, water was knee-deep on the lot after the matinee. The Labor Day stand was Memphis, Tennessee, and due to capacity limits, many in the crowd had to be turned away at both afternoon and night performances. Cotter, Arkansas, was the smallest town played and only an afternoon performance was given, but to a big audience. In all, the show covered sixteen states, playing forty-two stands in Ohio alone.

In the 1911 menagerie, there were nine elephants. The largest was Bazil, who had been with the show forty years. Camels, sacred cattle and seventeen cages and dens of assorted animals were also included. The cages were as large and costly as any in the business, and they were painted by skilled artists. Crowds lined the streets of every town and city, eager to see the street parade. All the cages in the parade were drawn by teams of four or six dun, gray and black horses, with brass studded harnesses and trappings. Two elaborate band wagons with heavy carvings were in the line with the Golden Peacock leading and drawn by twelve black horses with enamel trappings and waving plumes, preceded by six lady and gent buglers in purple robes

The ornate Golden Dragon bandwagon and band. 1906. *University of Cincinnati Library Archive.*

riding dun horses. There was a mounted band, the eight Holloway brothers, who were also ushers in the big show.

The 1911 season proved very pleasant and profitable, closing in New Albany, Mississippi, on November 16. That was the final year of the show under the ownership and management of the Ohio-based Robinson family.

CHAPTER 3

THE SELLS BROTHERS CIRCUS OF CENTRAL OHIO

In 1872, a circus was organized in Columbus, Ohio, that became one of the premier shows of all time. The circus toured continuously for nearly thirty-five years. During this time, it also sometimes operated a second unit, all of which brought wealth to the men whose name it headlined, the Sells Brothers. The Sells name is one of the most respected in the American circus business.

The original Sells family had eleven children, which included six sons. As was typical in the mid-nineteenth century, five of the sons fought for the Union. One brother died during the Civil War in the dreaded Confederate Andersonville prison. Another was shot and killed while on duty as a guard at the Ohio State Penitentiary in Columbus. The four remaining sons, Ephraim (1834–1898), Allen (1836–1894), Lewis (1841–1907) and Peter (1845–1904), would eventually establish the renowned circus.

Prior to the Civil War, the four brothers all worked around Columbus. Allen worked at gardening with his father, Peter Sr.; Ephraim got married and went to Cleveland, where he established a truck garden; Lewis later joined Ephraim in Cleveland. Lewis then accepted a position with James Anderson as a driver and conductor on a streetcar line in Cleveland. Anderson would later become part of the Sells circus organization.

William Kent, an uncle of the Sells brothers', operated an auction house in Columbus and engaged Lewis to help him. Lewis learned the business quickly and soon interested his brothers Ephraim and Allen in starting their own auction house. The business prospered initially, but in order to sell their

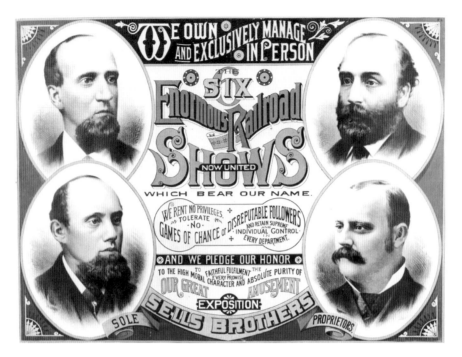

Early poster depicting all four Sells brothers, *from top left to right*, Ephraim, Allen, Lewis and Peter Sells. Circa 1880. *State Library of Ohio.*

surplus stock, the brothers started traveling as auctioneers and often followed circus troupes to take advantage of the general gathering of the crowds. The idea of going into the circus business first occurred to Allen, and he also urged Lewis to do the same.

During the winter of 1867, the Sells brothers were operating a small auction house in Burlington, Iowa. While there, they decided to make their first attempt at establishing a circus. This was a brief and unprofitable association with James T. Johnson in a hippodrome. This short exposure brought no profit, but Allen remained enthusiastic. So in the winter of 1871, Allen and his friend George Richards, a cannonball performer, talked Lewis into buying some secondhand circus equipment that also included a few animals. In November 1871, Lewis Sells went to Cincinnati to attend an auction of equipment and animals from the Madame Lake Circus and the Colonel Ames Menagerie. There, he purchased a tired grizzly bear for $350, a camel for $410 and four lion cubs for $860. At that time Peter was still employed as a reporter for the *Ohio State Journal* in Columbus, but he also became a working partner in the undertaking. The initial 1872 spring show was presented in downtown Columbus at the corner lot of State and High Streets. The show consisted of one tent for a small menagerie, Cannonball George Richards, a few sideshow features and traveled by horses and wagons. The circus prospered to the extent that the brothers were able to expand their operation the following season. They invested about $6,500 ($135,000 in 2018 dollars), which represented all of their savings and a loan.

The circus opened on April 19, 1872, and was billed as the Paul Silverburg Mammoth Quadruple Alliance, Museum, Menagerie, Caravan and Circus. Apparently, they felt the name Paul Silverburg sounded more like an older, well-established show from an East Coast city. The show carried nineteen baggage wagons, thirteen cages, a tableau wagon, 130 horses and a camel. The gross receipts for opening day were $1,540 ($32,000 in 2018 dollars), even though it was a wet day. But business did not continue on that scale, and in time it was necessary for Ephraim to return to Columbus and borrow more money to keep operating. But the season was completed. It was reasoned that what really contributed to the lack of real success was that their show didn't have an elephant. So as a result, an elephant was acquired for the next season.

The 1873 season opened on April 19 and 21, a Saturday and Monday, in Columbus. The advertisement in the *Ohio State Journal* carried the billing of Sells Brothers Mammoth Quadruple Alliance Combined with Paul Silverburg's Monster Menagerie, Museum, Aviary, Roman Hippodrome, Oriental Caravan and Trans Atlantic Circus. This variation of the billing was common with the show during the first three years. As evidenced by newspaper ads, the different variations would be used in different towns during the same season. A handwritten route kept by Orrin L. Hollis, a bareback rider, shows that the show remained in Ohio and Kentucky for the full tour and closed on August 30 in Guthrie, Kentucky. The early season closing was because the bank in Columbus that held the Sells brothers' savings had failed. So they immediately returned to their winter headquarters in Columbus. Even with a short season, the show proved successful. The elephant purchased in the spring proved to be a very presentable crowd-pleaser. In general, the show traveled an average of fifteen miles a day, with the longest trek being twenty-four miles in one day. In all, the show logged 1,741 miles that season.

In time, the Sells brothers dropped the Silverburg label, and on April 16, 1874, they opened with a three-day stand in Columbus as the Great European Zoological Association, British Museum and Royal Coliseum, under immediate supervision of the Sells brothers. The "zoological" title was used with slight variations for the 1875, 1876 and 1877 seasons. During this time, the show prospered and was expanded each season.

In February 1878, the Sells brothers purchased a large part of the bankrupt Montgomery Queen Railroad Circus and Menagerie. This enabled them to make two major moves in the expansion of their operations. First, they switched to rail transportation, using the Montgomery Queen equipment, and called the show Sells Brothers Great European Seven Elephant Show (the Barnum and the Cooper & Bailey shows had only six elephants at the time). The second big move that season was to establish a second unit, a wagon show, probably using the old Sells equipment, called Anderson & Company's Great World's Circus and Menagerie, under the management of James P. Anderson, who had previously been the Sells show contracting agent.

The "Seven Elephant Show" included eighteen flats, seven stock cars, two elephant cars, five coaches and two advance advertising cars. The railcars were manufactured in Chicago, Illinois, by the United States Rolling Stock Company. Fully assembled and outfitted, the trains made a grand impression rolling over the steel rails from town to town. The special season opened in Columbus on April 20 and 22 and closed at a return stand in Columbus on October 27. The brothers' duties were divided as follows: Allen Sells was the manager; Lewis was assistant manager and superintendent; Ephraim was treasurer and superintendent of tickets; and Peter traveled ahead as router and advertiser, and later as railroad contractor. Early in the season, the show suffered a train wreck on the way to London, Kentucky. The train was moving in two sections and the second section telescoped into the first, resulting in two employees and a number of horses killed. But the season ended well, in black ink, and clearly demonstrated the advantage of rail travel versus horse and wagon. The staff was better rested and ready for the next town performance.

The season of 1880 was titled the Sells Brothers Great European Millionaire Museum, Menagerie, Circus and Stupendous Confederation of Railroad Shows. That particular year saw 10,752 miles traveled throughout the North and South by rail and a return to Columbus in early November. On April 21, upon the show arriving in Kansas City and after setting up the canvas tent, high winds started that made it impossible to have a show. The canvas was taken down and the entire operation moved on to the next scheduled town with the idea of returning to Kansas City later in the season. Also in 1880, the Anderson show was renamed the New Pacific Circus and Menagerie. The Welch & Sands title was also used on some dates. Lewis

Forepaugh Sells elephants being carefully unloaded from a railcar. Circa 1900. *Western Reserve Historical Society.*

was placed in charge of the second show, and the show did well under his management.

During the 1881 Sells circus season, on May 2 in St. Louis, Missouri, there was no show given because it had rained extremely hard all day. On that same day, a giraffe was added to the menagerie but unfortunately it died upon arrival. But five day later on May 7, another giraffe arrived alive and well and was added to the menagerie. On June 11, high winds interfered with giving a performance in Creston, Iowa. The center pole in the ladies' dressing room broke as they were getting ready for the street parade. And just prior to the afternoon show, the wind ripped the circus big top into fragments, causing a general panic. People rushed down off the seats and out from under the tent sidewalls. After a little time, calm was restored and the audience members returned to the tent and their seats. The concert and circus performance proceeded as planned. The evening performance was given under the open sky without a top in place. In Circleville, Ohio, on July 9, the mandrill died. This death was a severe blow to the menagerie, as it was one of the rarest species of the animal kingdom and the largest primate of the monkey family and featured a rainbow of facial colors.

Above: Sells Circus Giraffe Wagon prepped for railroad travel. Circa 1898. *Kansas City, Kansas Public Library.*

Opposite, top: S.H. Barrett's Circus and Menagerie. Sheldon Hopkins Barrett was a brother-in-law to the Sells brothers. Idaletta & Wallace Troupe Aerialist. Circa 1880. *Oregon State Archive.*

Opposite, bottom: Poster ad of Willie Sells, who was an equestrian and the adopted son of Allen Sells. Circa 1880. *Cincinnati Art Museum.*

In 1882, the second show was placed on rails under the name S.H. Barrett's Circus and Menagerie. Sheldon Hopkins Barrett was a brother-in-law of the Sells brothers', married to their sister Rebecca, and also served as their general agent. New rail equipment was purchased for the Sells show and the old equipment was used to put the Barrett show on rails.

The 1882 season opened in Columbus to a crowd of over eight thousand people. In Kansas City, Missouri, on May 8, the audience was favored with a visit from the brothers Charley and Robert Ford. A month previously, they had gained national fame by shooting the unarmed Jesse James, the noted outlaw, in the back of the head and killing him. The death of Jesse James became a national sensation. The Fords made no attempt to hide their roles. Robert Ford wired the Missouri governor to claim his reward as there was a bounty on James. On May 11, the show pulled into St. Joseph, Missouri, which was the home of Jesses James. Several members of the staff paid twenty-five cents to receive a tour of James's home. They were taken to the room where the killing took place five weeks earlier and were given all the details of the legendary event.

On June 15 as the train was passing through Stillwater, Iowa, it was discovered upon opening the cage containing the lions that the lioness and three new cubs had died during the night. This was another terrible loss to the menagerie.

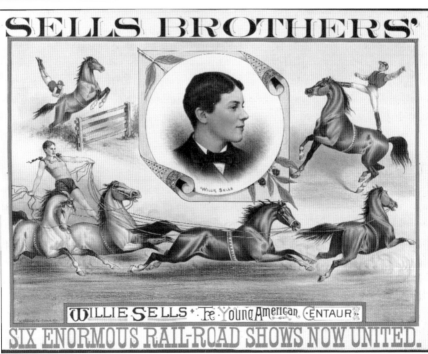

Although better equipped, and playing the larger towns under Ephraim's supervision, the show was not seeing near the profits that the S.H. Barrett show was making playing the country towns under Lewis's guidance. Ephraim was a very competent treasurer and on the job every minute, but he did not have the comprehensive ability and vision a manager should have. But his son, Allen E. Sells, made a good superintendent under him.

It should be noted that during 1882, before the Ringling brothers created their first circus, the six brothers—Alf, Al, Gus, Charles, Otto and John Ringling—performed skits and juggling routines in town halls around the state of Wisconsin. Their first show was presented in Mazomanie, Wisconsin, on November 27, 1882. They expanded their acts into a one-ring show in 1884. The show added a trick horse and a bear toward the end of the season. The circus didn't start traveling by trains until 1888, a full decade after the Sells Brothers Circus.

Allen Sells grew tired of the circus business in 1883 and sold out to his brothers and proceeded to go into the hotel business in Topeka, Kansas. Allen's adopted son, Willie Sells, remained with the show as a star equestrian rider. The following year, the Sells show title was extended to include "Fifty Cage Menagerie and Four-Ring Circus." The expanded exhibit of animals was extensively advertised. Although many of the cages were

A rare photo of a worker holding a lion by the tail as it is being transferred from a railcar to another cage wagon. Circa 1895. *Washington County Ohio Historical Society.*

The Sells Circus had several Bactrian camels in its menagerie. Circa 1890. *Washington County Ohio Historical Society.*

small and could be loaded cross-wise on the rail-flats, the show did have the advertised number of animal dens. These were paraded open and shown in the menagerie. The season opened in Columbus on April 16 and closed in New Orleans, Louisiana, on December 8. Total mileage for the season was 11,537. During that period, both the Sells and Barrett shows were on the road. Both presented a fine spread of canvas and were moved on from forty to fifty railcars.

The Sells Brothers Circus over the years became the strongest in the territory from Ohio west to the plains area of Kansas, Iowa and Nebraska. Periodically, they would venture toward the East Coast into the Maryland area but did not venture into the Barnum and Forepaugh territory of New England until later years. They also went farther west on occasion, playing the coastal area of California in 1891.

In the late nineteenth century, operating a successful, large-scale circus show required a person that was good at what is known in the twenty-first

Sell Brothers Fife & Drum Corps. Circa 1890. *Chillicothe and Ross County Public Library.*

A crowd would generally gather once news got out that the Forepaugh-Sells train had arrived in town. Circa 1904. *Dayton and Montgomery County Library.*

century as multitasking. Most folks imagine a boss showman in those days had nothing to do but sit in big leather chairs in hotel corridors and decline to be interviewed, while leaving all the hard work of the show to all his lieutenants. In an article that appeared in *Collier's* weekly, Peter Sells states that in truth a circus proprietor must know more and work harder than anyone in his employ:

Even if he cannot do stunts in the ring himself, he needs to know how each particular performer should execute their act. He must be omniscient. He must know all about wild animals, their haunts, habits, food and cost of caring for the animals properly. Circus owners should be acquainted with what kinds of hides are required to make different types of harnesses and should know every point of every horse, from draft to a thoroughbred. Regarding maintenance he should have a thorough knowledge of painting and the value of paints, color pigments and oils. Also important is knowledge of feedstuffs for every description of man and beast from different continents. He must be a veterinarian, a printer, papermaker and lithographer. He should be familiar with when crops are being harvested and sold in all parts of the country and must be acquainted with the industries of the different parts of every state in the Union. It is very important to know the dates when employees are paid off and know the art of advertising in all its branches and the relative value of notices in the principal newspapers in every city and town. And it is crucial that he stay up to date about municipal ordinances, legislation and license laws that apply to the circus business in all cities.

Then there is the need to know all about railroading, from scheduling and track size in different parts of the country to the way a railcar is constructed and the science of transportation on land and sea. Above all, he must know that it is no longer possible to humbug the public.

These are just a few things that Peter Sells made a point of knowing in the course of his circus career. Between accidents, delays and other losses, he discovered the disadvantage of not knowing things. In the same *Collier's* article, Sells tells of one particular incident, stating,

I remember an instance in 1882, when circuses were new to railroads because until a few years before shows were hauled about the country by horses and wagons. Our train pulled within sight of Columbia, South Carolina, and then suddenly stopped! We were at the end of a bridge which was too small to admit the cars containing our wagons. As we were obliged to continue the journey south over that road, we had to make a detour of two hundred and fifty miles and lost the stand in Columbia because I had failed to inform myself regarding the height of that one bridge.

In order to stay on top in the circus business, you have to stay ahead of your competition. So in May 1886, Allen Sells and Budd Gorman visited the W.W. Cole Circus as spectators—or spies. Upon their return, they both spoke highly of the Cole show and were impressed. In the next month, Ephraim Sells and a close associate also paid a visit to the Cole Circus that was also playing in Nebraska and were surprisingly impressed. This sparked the imaginations of the Sells brothers and staff to be extra-creative in planning how to impress and catch the public's attention. The Sells show presented many of the outstanding performing names of the day, such as James Robinson and Orrin Hollis.

Anxious to be at the top, the Sells show in 1887 featured a Grand Firemen's Tournament, which pitted the show's fire company against any local competitors in the hook and ladder category, with the winner receiving a "solid silver goblet." It is not known if this trophy ever left the show's ownership, but local judges did conduct the race. In Indiana, according to the *Fort Wayne Weekly Sentinel*, "a soul stirring artillery race, depicting the famous episode at the Battle of Shiloh," was also a feature in 1887. But the biggest feature in the 1887 show was Pawnee Bill's Historical Wild West.

Sells Brothers circus presents Professor Merrick and his band with old-fashioned tableau wagons in the background. 1889. *Dayton and Montgomery County Library.*

Sells Brothers steam calliope in street parade. Circa 1890. *Chillicothe and Ross County Public Library.*

The Sells brothers had watched with interest the attention being given by the public to the Wild West exhibitions performed by Buffalo Bill and Colonel Carver starting in 1883. The Sells show decided to add a Wild West department to its circus for the season of 1887 and engaged Major Gordon W. Lillie, a.k.a. Pawnee Bill. They met with Lillie in Allen Sells's hotel in Topeka and contracted with him to furnish Native Americans, cowboys and all equipment necessary for a complete Wild West exhibition to be featured in 1887.

Extensive special advertising was prepared in large quantities, and the advertising crews began their publicity campaign for the season's opening. Major Lillie went to a reservation to hire Native Americans and transport them to the show as he had done in previous years for other shows. He had no problem in arranging all the details, but his plans were undermined by a recent federal order preventing the transport of Native Americans from reservations for entertainment purposes. Federal agents arrested Lillie. He was detained several days, during which time the Native Americans he planned to hire were signed up by another medicine show.

Forepaugh Sells featuring the Hales Fire Fighters spectacle. Circa 1906. *Oregon State Archive.*

Kids watching circus setup and staging on the lot. Circa 1890. *Greene County Ohio Historical Society.*

He went to the show and prepared for the season's engagement with a Mexican cast, cowboys and all the equipment needed for the Pawnee Bill Wild West exhibition, but with no Native Americans. The circus owners were not impressed by his story of the federal order, seeing it as an excuse for not delivering as agreed. There was also considerable friction over the delay in getting the Wild West performance started on opening day. The other performers made fun of the Wild West staff, and a number of fights resulted. This situation was taken advantage of by the Sells management, and fines were assessed against the cowboys and Mexican cast and deducted from Major Lillie on salary days. The fines increased until they became a burden, and Lillie finally gave his two-week notice and left the show.

Sells Brothers, in an effort to continue the Wild West features after Lillie left, used other staff, in makeup and costumes, to play the roles of cowboys, Mexicans and Native Americans. The show had staff doing Wild West stunts with considerable shooting using blank cartridges, but it was a poor imitation of the Pawnee Bill show. This ended in tragedy that eventually cost the Sells brothers a lot of money. On the day after Lillie left, some of the amateur Wild West actors put on their performance on July 19 in Clinton, Iowa. A mistake was made in loading one of the pistols with real bullets (instead of blank cartridges) that were fired and caused serious injury to three people in the audience. One of the victims was the wife of the local county attorney. In the excitement that followed, the circus was hastily dismantled and loaded, and the train left the state entirely, blowing the next day's stand. The route was resumed in Wisconsin, but for several years, Sells Brothers made a point not to include Iowa in its route planning, and eventually damage claims against the show were settled for a substantial amount. Pawnee Bill started his own show the following year.

The Sells show and the Barrett show represented an extremely large amount of equipment and gear in addition to their large assortment of animals. If the two shows based in Columbus, Ohio, were combined, it would have been the third-largest circus show in the country and rivaled only by Barnum & Bailey and Adam Forepaugh for bragging sake, on "Earth." The Sells brothers were very able showmen but when divided didn't function quite as well as a management team. After Allen's departure, Lewis Sells became the directing officer. He was a competent director with the original show, but now he switched his attention to the Barrett division and a strong hand was needed for the Sells brothers' number one show. Peter Sells handled only advance logistics and didn't care for general

Cook tent with surplus bread fed to some animals later. Circa 1890. *Kansas City, Kansas Public Library.*

on-site show operations. The S.H. Barrett show division continued to be more profitable to the point that serious dissension developed at the close of the 1887 season.

The year 1888 saw the S.H. Barrett show taken off the road and its title was combined with Sells for a single show. The title used by the show from 1888 to 1890 was "Sells Brothers Enormous Roman Hippodrome Double Elevated Stage and Five Continent Menagerie, United with S H. Barrett's Monster World's Fair." A great portion of the property was sold, after the best from both shows had been selected for the new organization. Lewis Sells now served as general director of the combined show. Interestingly, during this time the Ringling brothers were still a wagon road show and had acquired their first elephant from an auction sale.

In 1889, the Sells Brothers Enormous United Shows with S.H. Barrett's Monster Consolidated Show began the season from the winter quarters at Stockton, California. On March 31, while on a run to Lathrop, California, as the train was rounding a curve, car no. 1 ran off the track and into a ditch.

This was caused by the rails spreading due to the weight and speed of the train at the curve.

In San Francisco on April 27, the evening show opened to a full house. That same day, the Society of California Pioneers prevented the Japanese children from performing because they did not want any of their local funds going to Asians.

On July 22, just as the train was two miles from Montpelier, Idaho, an axle broke on a ring equipment car, causing it and the horse car behind it to break down directly on the tracks. Several horses were bruised but not seriously injured.

While the show was in Chillicothe, Missouri, on September 2, the city tax collector, a Mr. Campbell, drove by the circus show grounds with his wife and child. Their horse caught the scent of the various animals in the menagerie and proceeded to erratically run away, throwing Mr. Campbell out of the buggy. He suffered a fractured skull and as a result died two hours later. Since this was a very out-of-the-ordinary event, the circus was not held responsible.

With good management, the next few years saw excellent returns, and strategic planning for a foreign tour was in the works. The show was routed to California in 1891 and closed the regular season in San Francisco. The circus was loaded onto a steam freighter and arrived in Sydney, Australia, on November 12, 1891. The stock was at once quarantined for a period of sixty

Japanese Troupe was an audience favorite because of the members' exceptional skill and colorful presentation. Circa 1890. *Washington County Ohio Historical Society.*

days due to an epidemic of glanders, which is a contagious disease that mainly affects horses. The show attempted after a few weeks to operate with newly purchased stock but this effort was not successful. By the time the horses were returned to the show, a lot of time and money had been lost and the tour, in general, was a failure. Australian officials played a part in undermining the show because they wanted local circuses to maintain their advantage. A local health inspector in Australia initially approved the Sells livestock for entry and within hours changed his declaration, according to Sells tour management. And everything that followed worked against their realizing a profit. Sells was the third large American show to play that continent, and the tour in no way measured up to the projections of the management.

The show returned to San Francisco, arriving June 9, 1892. It opened the 1892 American tour in San Francisco, running from June 15 to 26, and made its way through California, Arizona, Texas, New Mexico, Colorado, Kansas, Missouri, Illinois, Indiana, Ohio (Columbus, the winter quarters city, was played on August 24), West Virginia and Kentucky. The show then headed back into Indiana and Illinois. A tour of the South was made in the fall, with the season closing in Gadsden, Alabama, on November 15.

When the show returned to the Columbus winter headquarters, it had traveled a total of 41,145 miles since leaving in the spring of 1891. This

The Sells Brothers Circus Australia Tour group and management staff. 1891. *Library of Congress.*

Sells Brothers cast included a very tall gentleman contrasted with a very short lady; both were part of the 1891 Australian tour. *Library of Congress.*

included 14,400 miles to Australia and back. The S.H. Barrett title was dropped for the Australian tour and the American tour of 1892. The Sells Brothers show never really regained its former success, and it was not able to recoup the losses from the foreign tour.

By 1890, the Ringling show had moved into the big leagues by going on rails and in the next few years became very strong in the "wheat and corn belt" that had been the Sells circus's best territory. Ringling was able to take full advantage of the Sells show being out of the country. After the Sells circus returned from Australia, the Sells and Ringling shows declared war on each other for the best spots in the Midwest. But the Sells show was the loser and was forced to invade New England for the 1895 season. The show quickly traveled east that year, playing Dunkirk, New York, on May 23, and after playing both the New England and New York areas, the Sells circus headed into Canada. There, it played a stand at St. John, New Brunswick, on July 22. The show returned to the United States via Niagara Falls on September 8 and headed south to the "cotton belt" for a tour that wrapped up the season in Cedartown, Georgia, on November 30.

Competing with the now formidable Ringling Bros. show placed the Sells Circus in a position that required the owners to seek a business ally. In 1896, James A. Bailey, who previously had been the one person the Sells brothers were constantly trying to stay ahead of in business, acquired a one-third ownership of the show. This then provided the needed operating capital and the right to use the valuable "Adam Forepaugh" title, which Bailey also owned. The combined show opened in 1896 on fifty railcars loaded completely with Sells equipment, aside from the old Forepaugh Cleopatra Barge Float and two former telescoping tableaux originally from the 1871 Howes Great London Circus.

The show moved in three sections in 1896, made up as follows: The first section included five stock railcars, eight flats, Ephraim Sells's private car for the five bosses and the canvas man, one boxcar and one sleeping combined car, making a total of sixteen railcars. The second section consisted of sixteen total boxcars; and the third section was made up of a camel car, two elephant cars, eight flats, three sleepers and one boxcar, making fifteen total cars in this section. The 1896 season Sells elephants were Mike and Topsy (both Africans), Sid, Queen, Dutch, Babe, Rubber, Betts, Romeo, Vic, Dick and John (all Asiatic). Other lead stock on the show included one zebra, one llama, seven camels and four ostriches.

The big top was a 178-foot round top, with three 50-foot middle poles and one 60-foot middle. There were seventy lengths of blue seating and

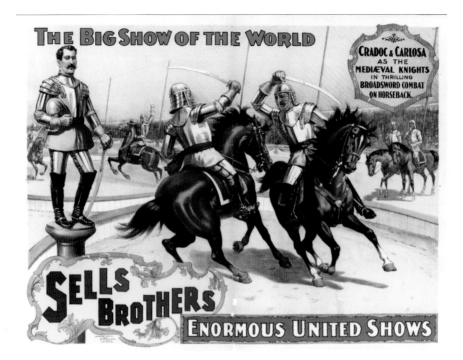

Above: Sells Brothers Circus *presents Cardoc & Carlosa as Knights in armor. Circa 1895.* Printed by the Strobridge Lithographing Company. *Cincinnati Art Museum.*

Right: Sells brothers Ephraim, Lewis and Peter Sells Sole Proprietors. Circa 1885. *Printed by the Strobridge Lithographing Company. Cincinnati Art Museum.*

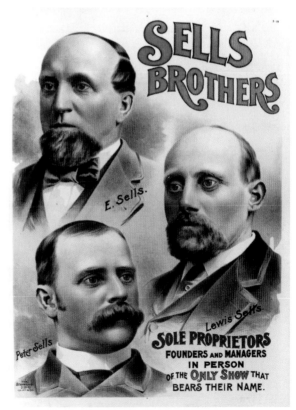

Above: Sells Brothers Enormous United Shows Bare Back Roman Standing Races. Circa 1889. *Printed by the Strobridge Lithographing Company. Cincinnati Art Museum.*

Left: Sells Brothers Enormous United Shows. Rare Zoological Marvels. A Grand 5 Continent Menagerie. Circa 1888. *Printed by the Strobridge Lithographing Company. Cincinnati Art Museum.*

Adam Forepaugh & Sells Brothers presents the Carl Damann Family of Acrobats. 1898. *Printed by the Strobridge Lithographing Company. Cincinnati Art Museum.*

Walter L. Main Shows; Wheelbarrow Races. Circa 1895. *Printed by Courier Lithograph Company. Ashtabula Ohio County Library.*

Sells Brothers Lions of the Ocean from the Frozen Zone. Circa 1888. *Printed by the Strobridge Lithographing Company. Cincinnati Art Museum.*

Sell Brothers Interior Pageant and Oriental Entrée! Circa 1880. *Printed by the Strobridge Lithographing Company. Cincinnati Art Museum.*

Right: Sells Brothers features Mr. William Showles and Miss Daisy Belmont. Circa 1890. *Printed by the Strobridge Lithographing Company. Cincinnati Art Museum.*

Below: Sells Brothers featuring W.H. Gorman & Polly Lee Equestrian Acts. Circa 1888. *Printed by the Strobridge Lithographing Company. Cincinnati Art Museum.*

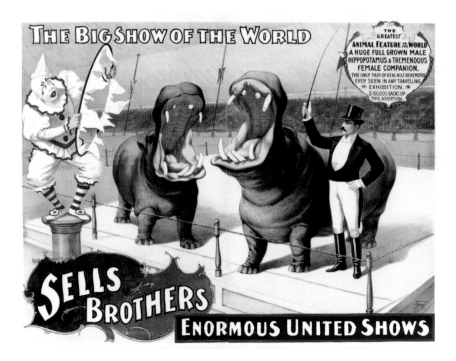

Above: Sells Brothers The Greatest Animal Feature in the World; Male and Female Hippos. Circa 1890. *Printed by the Strobridge Lithographing Company. Cincinnati Art Museum.*

Left: Sells Brothers Just Returned from Australia. Featuring Billy Carroll & Brother Clown Act combined with Hassab Ben Ali's Moorish Caravan. Circa 1894. *Printed by the Strobridge Lithographing Company. Cincinnati Art Museum.*

Right: Sells Brothers featuring Ottoe and Higo's Acrobatic Exhibitions. Circa 1885. *Printed by the Strobridge Lithographing Company. Cincinnati Art Museum.*

Below: Sells Brothers featuring six open dens of performing wild beasts and crocodiles. Circa 1885. *Printed by the Strobridge Lithographing Company. Cincinnati Art Museum.*

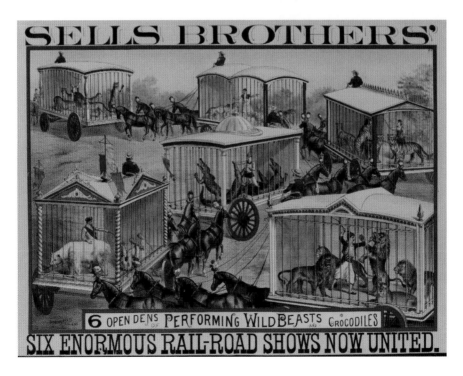

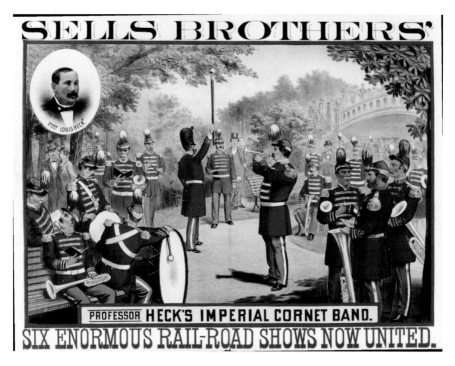

Sells Brothers featuring Professor Heck's Imperial Cornet Band. Circa 1885. *Printed by the Strobridge Lithographing Company. Cincinnati Art Museum.*

Forepaugh Sells Aerial View of Combined Show Tent Lot. Circa 1897. *Printed by the Strobridge Lithographing Company. Cincinnati Art Museum.*

Above: Adam Forepaugh & Sells Brothers Giant Specimens of Rare Tropical and Arctic Animals such as Seals, Polar Bears and Hippos. Circa 1898. *Printed by the Strobridge Lithographing Company. Cincinnati Art Museum.*

Right: Sells Brothers Moorish Caravan; Pilgrimage to Mecca. Circa 1888. *Printed by the Strobridge Lithographing Company. Cincinnati Art Museum.*

Left: Sells Brothers featuring a pair of Diminutive Lilliputian Cattle. Circa 1885. *Printed by the Strobridge Lithographing Company. Cincinnati Art Museum.*

Below: S.H. Barrett & Company; Professor Harriman's Steam-Powered Airship. Circa 1895. *Printed by the Strobridge Lithographing Company. Cincinnati Art Museum.*

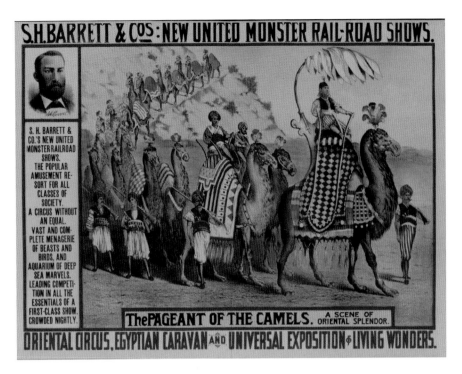

S.H Barrett & Co. New United Monster Railroad Shows; The Pageant of the Camels. Circa 1885. *Printed by the Strobridge Lithographing Company. Cincinnati Art Museum.*

Forepaugh & Sells Brothers Great Shows Consolidated at New York's Madison Square Garden. Circa 1900. *Printed by the Strobridge Lithographing Company. Cincinnati Art Museum.*

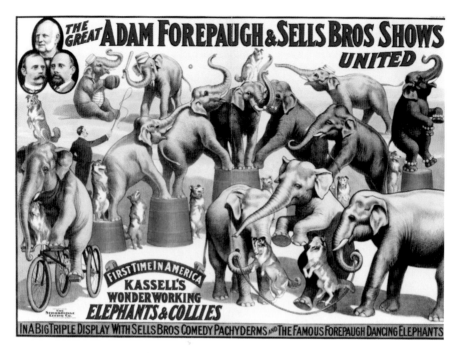

The Great Adam Forepaugh & Sells Bros. Shows United presents Kassell's Wonderworking Elephants & Collies. Circa 1899. *Printed by the Strobridge Lithographing Company. Cincinnati Art Museum.*

The Great Adam Forepaugh & Sells Bros. Shows featuring a wide variety of comic and clown acts. Circa 1890. *Printed by the Strobridge Lithographing Company. Cincinnati Art Museum.*

Sells Brothers Enormous United Shows featuring the Mighty Cradoc performing with axes. Circa 1890. *Printed by the Strobridge Lithographing Company. Cincinnati Art Museum.*

Sells Brothers featuring gymnasts the Wonderful French Family Davene. Circa 1900. *Printed by the Strobridge Lithographing Company. Cincinnati Art Museum.*

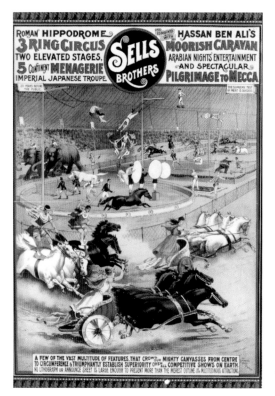

Sells Brothers presents a Roman Hippodrome featuring a Ladies Chariot Race. Circa 1889. *Printed by the Strobridge Lithographing Company. Cincinnati Art Museum.*

"Just Returned from Australia." A Whole Menagerie and Aviary of Recently Imported Australian Animals such as platypuses, kangaroos, birds and snakes in the wild. 1893. *Cincinnati Art Museum.*

Right: Buffalo Bill Cody
ad poster produced by
Russell-Morgan printers of
Cincinnati, Ohio. Circa 1900.
Library of Congress.

Below: S.H. Barrett & Co. New
United Monster Railroad
Shows; The Young American
Equestrian, Orrin Hollis. Circa
1885. *Printed by the Strobridge
Lithographing Company. Cincinnati
Art Museum.*

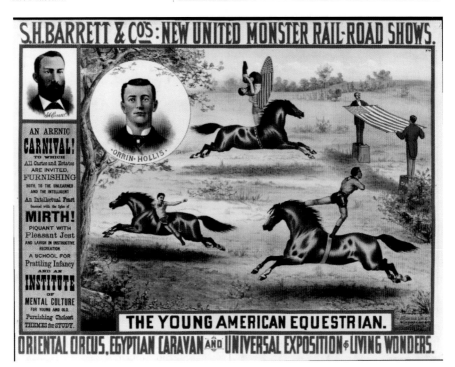

Adam Forepaugh & Sells Brothers presents a herd of trained elephants performing various tricks in the center ring. 1899. *Printed by the Strobridge Lithographing Company. Cincinnati Art Museum.*

Adam Forepaugh & Sells Brothers presents horse trainer Daniel Curtis and his center ring performance involving sixty horses. 1898. *Printed by the Strobridge Lithographing Company. Cincinnati Art Museum.*

Sell Brothers Circus ticket booth was also equipped with a safe to keep the daily cash proceeds. Circa 1890. *Washington County Ohio Historical Society.*

Forepaugh-Sells management staff standing in front of a sleeper car. Circa 1900. *Cincinnati & Hamilton County Library.*

seventeen lengths of reserve seats as well as fifty-nine lengths of extra red seats. The sideshow top was a 60-foot round top with two 28-foot middle poles. It had three 28-foot center poles, ten 19-foot quarter poles and thirty-two 12-foot side poles. The fourteen banners required fifteen 21-foot poles. Other sideshow equipment included fourteen stages with jacks, carpets and screens, two dressing room screens, bandstand with jacks and planks and three ticket boxes.

The sideshow features, under manager Thomas B. McIntyre, were G.A. Shields and wife, giants ($35 a week or $1,000 in 2018 dollars); Wesley Baum and wife, tattooed people ($20 a week or $600 in 2018 dollars); William Parkinson, magician and inside lecturer ($45 a week or $1,350 in 2018 dollars); Willie Ray and wife, midgets ($30 a week or $900 in 2018 dollars);

Forepaugh-Sells menagerie tent interior with cage wagons. Circa 1900. *Cincinnati & Hamilton County Library.*

Forepaugh-Sells interior view of the big top. Circa 1900. *Cincinnati & Hamilton County Library.*

Nettie Leona, snake charmer ($15 a week or $450 in 2018 dollars); W.H. McFarland and wife, outside opening and knife throwing ($40 a week or $1,200 in 2018 dollars), and the Hindoo giants and wives ($20 total). In addition, one man was paid $5 a week to have rocks broken on his head and another also received $5 to be a wild man.

A minstrel performance was presented with sixteen African Americans that included a band of six. Solomon White was the sideshow bandleader and was paid $80 a week (or $2,400 in 2018 dollars), including the band. There were four "orators," or ticket sellers, ranging in salary from $25 to $12 a week. Total cost for the sideshow was $282 (or $8,400 in 2018 dollars).

In addition to the canvas mentioned above, the show carried seven five-pole horse tents and two seven-pole horse tents. A total of 245 head of horses were stabled, of which 191 were baggage stock, divided into two ten, two eight, twelve six and fourteen four horse teams.

The show carried 332 working men and 64 performers. The total weekly cost for the performers was $1,979.35 ($60,000 in 2018 dollars). The highest-paid act was the diversely talented Stirk Family of twelve, who received $300 a week ($9,000 in 2018 dollars). They did a bicycle act, revolving trapeze, double contortion, flying rings, and tight wire, in addition to doing the "highland fling" in the concert. The next-highest-paid act, interestingly

Forepaugh-Sells talented general staff of show performers. Circa 1898. *Cincinnati & Hamilton County Library.*

enough, was the Woodwards and their trained seals and sea lions at $140 a week ($4,200 in 2018 dollars). The Dan Rhyan group of four received $135 a week ($4,000 in 2018 dollars) for an aerial act, clowning, Roman standing riding, driving chariot, leaps, tumbling and the old standby "being generally useful." The highest-paid individual-feature equestrian performers were Bud Gorman and his wife, Polly Lee, who were paid $100 a week ($3,000 in 2018 dollars).

There were nineteen men in the big show band, under leader T.B. Long, who was paid $30 a week ($900 in 2018 dollars). The musicians generally averaged $10 a week ($300 in 2018 dollars) for a total of $217 for the group. The big show band divided into first and second band sections for the parade.

For the 1896 season, Shelton H. Barrett was the general agent, with three advance advertising cars. The no. 1 advance advertising car, with H.I. Ellis as manager, carried a press agent, two lithographers, two programmers to distribute heralds and couriers and fourteen billposters. The no. 2 car, under F.W. Busey, manager, carried thirteen billposters and one lithographer.

Forepaugh-Sells Enormous Shows United presents Diavolo Looping the Loop. Circa 1900. *Printed by Strobridge Lithographing Company. Greene County Ohio Historical Society.*

The no. 3 car, with E.L. Bannon as manager, carried nine billposters. The amount of paper used each day during the 1896 season is not known, but a shipping list from the Strobridge Lithographing Company of Cincinnati to the Sells Circus for the 1893 season gives an idea of the amount of paper ordered for each day. In 1893, the show used forty-three different styles of posters, ranging from one to sixty-four sheets in size with each sheet measuring thirty inches by forty inches. For thirteen billing posters of a single style, two sheets were used. The big paste-up material daily order consisted of seven forty-eight sheets for the "Procession," seven forty-eight-sheet "Menagerie," three thirty-two-sheet "Arabs Performing," three thirty-two-sheet "Arab Pilgrimage," three twelve-sheet "Japanese," seven sixty-four-sheet "Circus and Hippodrome," three nine-sheet "Ostriches," seven twelve-sheet "Country Bill" and six twelve-sheet "Excursion Bill." All of this was either pasted or hung up each day.

The winter headquarters of the Sells Brothers Circus enterprise was northwest of downtown Columbus, Ohio, and grew to become one of the largest and finest in the country. Both the Sells Brothers and the S.H. Barrett shows wintered at this site. The Forepaugh-Sells show premiered for the first time under the new title in Columbus on April 21 and 22, 1896. It played Ohio and West Virginia and after showing in Pittsburgh on May 11 and 12, the show headed west for a stand in San Francisco from September 3 to the 12. While en route to San Francisco, the circus played stands in various states along the way. The show had managed to avoid confrontation with the Ringling show while moving west, but ran into the Wisconsin brothers on the way back into Texas. Dallas and Fort Worth were the focal points of the battle of Sells versus Ringling. Ringling got into town a week ahead of the Forepaugh-Sells Brothers show and showed to overflow audiences. The two crossed swords in San Antonio and Waco, along with a few other stands. During Sells's foreign-tour absence, the Ringlings were able to gain an advantage and move into a formidable position in the circus world and had no intentions of taking a back seat to anyone. The Forepaugh-Sells show moved east and through the South, closing at Charlotte, North Carolina, on November 21.

The 1897 season opened in Columbus on April 14 and 15, and the show moved quickly eastward, playing stands along the way and showing at Newark, New Jersey, on May 24. It stayed in the east until the middle of September and then hurried to move into Missouri and then into Texas for a late autumn tour. It closed in Texarkana, Texas, on December 3, for one of the longest seasons in its history. At the end of the season, James A. Bailey sold half of his one-sixth interest in the Forepaugh-Sells Brothers show so he and William W. Cole, a veteran circus man who also held a one-sixth interest, could have funding to take the Barnum & Bailey Circus on a European tour.

The 1898 season opened in Columbus, as usual, with a two-day stand on Monday and Tuesday, April 25 and 26. The show then moved through southern Ohio and played Charleston, West Virginia, on April 30. The Ringling show had opened in the St. Louis Coliseum for a comfortable April 11–20

The great circus entrepreneur Adam Forepaugh, partner with the Sells brothers. Circa 1898. *Western Reserve Historical Society.*

70

Forepaugh-Sells business staff. *Seated from left to right:* Lewis, Ephraim and Peter Sells. Circa 1896. *Dayton and Montgomery County Library.*

run indoors, and under canvas in Belleville, Illinois, on April 22. Ringling played Charleston a day ahead of Forepaugh-Sells Brothers on April 29. The advance billing opposition between the shows was extremely intense. Ringling's 1898 route book has little to say about business that day, but the Sells show recorded a big day according to its route book. The feeling between the shows is illustrated by this quotation from the Forepaugh-Sells Brothers 1898 route book: "Had the opposition been a really first class show, the Forepaugh-Sells Brothers victory in Charleston would have been great. An elephant gains little glory in besting an ant." The show moved back into Ohio and on to Chicago for six days. The Chicago stand was big and compared strongly with the Barnum & Bailey show the year before. The show continued through Wisconsin and on to Minnesota and the Dakotas, before moving into its home ground in the Nebraska, Iowa, and Missouri area. In Iowa, it again ran into the "Ding-Dong" brothers from "Bugaboo," as they were referred to in the Forepaugh-Sells Brothers route book. Waterloo on July 9 had the Forepaugh-Sells Brothers show, with Ringling in a week earlier at nearby Cedar Falls. The Ringling show was then routed west, and Forepaugh-Sells Brothers proceeded eastward.

On July 30, 1898, it was announced on the show that Ephraim Sells was in very grave condition, and his son, Allen E., left for Columbus to be with his father. Louis Sells followed the next day, and both were at Ephraim's side when he died on August 1. The show closed the season in Danville, Virginia, on November 24.

Following the death of Ephraim Sells, the ownership of the circus was redistributed to give Louis and Peter Sells, W.W. Cole and James A. Bailey each an equal one-quarter share. For the 1899 season, the show covered the eastern route of the Barnum & Bailey Circus that was now touring Europe in an attempt to outwit the Ringlings. The show opened in Madison Square Garden on April 18 and remained until the 29, and then went under canvas in Brooklyn for seven days, starting on May 1. But the going was rough during the 1899 season, and it did not appear that the Forepaugh-Sells Brothers name had the attention-getting luster it had in previous years. The situation became so bad that late in 1899, serious consideration was given to placing the Barnum & Bailey title on the Forepaugh-Sells Brothers equipment. Even though Bailey had the Barnum show in Europe, he had retained the American rights to the title. James A. Bailey returned to America to negotiate the matter, but soon headed back to London and left the dealings in the hands of a friend, Albert A. Stewart. After a month, the deal cooled off, mainly because of Peter Sells, who found himself involved in a very sensational and front-page divorce suit back in Columbus.

The show opened in New York at the Garden in 1900, 1901 and 1902 and continued over the old Barnum & Bailey route. The 1903 season opened under canvas in St. Louis after the Barnum & Bailey Circus returned to the United States.

Peter Sells had suffered a stroke at his Columbus home and died on the night of October 5, 1904, and this forced the sale of the circus to settle his estate. His entire estate, which included numerous other investments, was valued at close to $500,000 ($14 million in 2018 dollars). His estate was left to his daughter Florence, with a small bequest to each of his six surviving sisters. Peter's death also prompted Lewis Sells to retire at the end of the 1904 season.

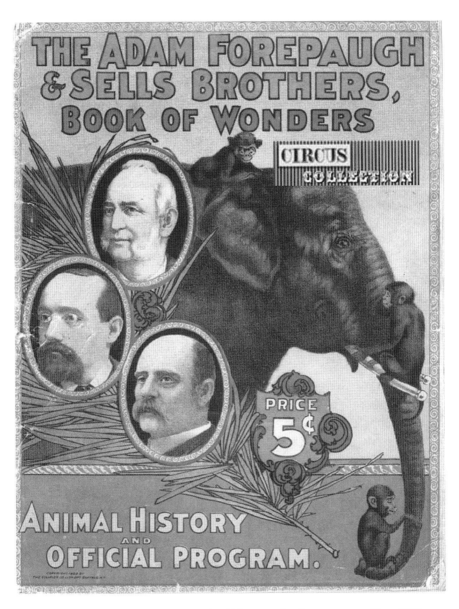

Forepaugh-Sells Book of Wonders included animal history and a show program. Circa 1900.
Grandview Heights Public Library.

Left: Portrait of Peter Sells, who was a master of circus advance logistics and promotion. Circa 1890. *Columbus Metropolitan Library.*

Right: Portrait of Lewis Sells, who was remembered in the circus business as a highly competent manager and show organizer. Circa 1890. *Columbus Metropolitan Library.*

Peter Sells's Columbus, Ohio home, located on Dennison Avenue, was built in 1895 in the Romanesque Revival architectural style and was designed by local architect Frank Packard. Circa 1898. *Columbus Metropolitan Library.*

Bailey had foreseen the time when he would have to assume management of the Forepaugh-Sells Brothers show and had asked his former associate and brother-in-law Joseph T. McCaddon to return as a manager. Needless to say, Bailey was somewhat boxed in, or he would never have resorted to calling upon McCaddon after only recently severing a long-term association. McCaddon passed up the offer, because he already committed himself to taking a show to Europe as the McCaddon International Circus. But this turned out to be a total failure.

As we look back on history, it is quite clear that Bailey had at this time decided that if he couldn't lick the opposition, he should join them. But Bailey kept a big front and announced that the Forepaugh-Sells Brothers show would be sold piecemeal at an auction on January 10, 1905, in Columbus, Ohio. Great publicity was given to the auction, and the owners even went so far as to issue a thirty-two-page catalog listing the equipment in detail. Circus owners came from all parts of the country. But as Richard Conover states in his book *The Affairs of James A. Bailey*, "The sale proved to be no more than a grand reunion of the big and little circus men who attended with the hopeful expectations of picking up some bargains."

With a call for bids from the auctioneer, Bailey immediately offered $150,000 for the complete show. Since there were no counter offers, that was the end of the auction. That same afternoon, he sat down for a prearranged meeting with the Ringlings and sold them one half of the show. The show was operated under the joint ownership during the 1905 season. On April 11, 1906, James A. Bailey died. On July 1, 1906, the Ringlings purchased Bailey's half interest in Forepaugh-Sells from his

Forepaugh-Sells in San Francisco shortly after the 1906 earthquake. *Fred Pfening Collection.*

widow, the former Ruth Louisa McCaddon from Zanesville, Ohio, for $50,000 ($1.4 million in 2018 dollars).

The Ringlings did not tour the show during the 1908 and 1909 season and had acquired the Barnum & Bailey show in 1907. In 1910, they revived the Forepaugh-Sells title for a smaller edition. The show's final tour was in 1911, and it was officially retired afterwards. But the Ringlings still held the rights to the renowned Sells name, along with the Forepaugh title. It was not until 1935 that the Sells name was again used, for the final time, in connection with the Hagenbeck-Wallace show.

Lewis Sells, who was by far the best executive of the four brothers, and counted as one of the most skillful and resourceful men in the circus world, died on September 5, 1907, at his home in Columbus, Ohio.

CHAPTER 4

THE WALTER L. MAIN HOMETOWN CIRCUS

Much of the following are recollections and remembrances of Walter L. Main and a number of his former employees as recorded by Louis E. Cooke in 1922. In his day, Cooke was a very well known advance agent for many of the high profile circus shows, including W.W. Cole, Adam Forepaugh, Buffalo Bill, Barnum & Bailey and Frank A. Robbins.

The story of Walter L. Main (1862–1950) starts out as a classic young farm boy sitting by the hearth or in the field listening to his elders exchange stories of their experiences at a sideshow or a small circus tent show given in the nearby towns. They were in awe of the fine horses with talented riders, daring trapeze performers, acrobats and clowns in flamboyant attire. These small, tented concerns would move from town to town by night, traveling by horse and wagon caravans. The tents were often set up in a vacant lot or town common.

Walter's father, William (Doctor) Main, was a sort of nonprofessional veterinarian or "horse doctor" for the Ashtabula County, Ohio area, and a horse trader by profession. He would periodically deal with traveling shows and once closed a horse deal with E.D. Colvin, an old-time circus man then traveling with the Van Amburgh show. It was at Paynesville, Ohio, in 1885 that this trade was transacted while the circus men were eating dinner in the cook tent. The animal that was offered for sale was led up to the opening where he could be seen. The animal appeared sleek and seemed to be a good specimen for baggage stock. Main and Colvin, who was the purchasing agent of the circus, quickly struck a deal. The showmen continued with their meal and asked not to be disturbed any further. The attendant was told to lead the animal back to the stable and turn him over to the boss hostler. Once dinner was completed, William Main was paid in cash. There was no further thought about the transaction or the horse until the teams were hitched up for the night haul to the show train. Then it was discovered that the glossy looking equine was so wind-broken that he wheezed and panted profusely when he stuck his head through the collar. This proved that William Main was one of the classic horse traders of legend.

William Main, with his own team of horses, obtained a job with Hilliard & Skinner's Variety and Indian show in 1872. This gave his son Walter, at age ten, an early opportunity to start learning firsthand the behind-the-scenes operations and logistics of a circus.

In 1873, William Main traveled with Hamilton, Blanchard & Carver's Wagon Circus. He furnished his own services and four horses to haul the bandwagon, and there were about forty horses with the outfit all told. The show opened in Windsor, Ohio, and Walter walked from Trumbull to Windsor and returned disappointed that the show had no riding acts. The season continued with varied success and closed at Fort Scott, Kansas. The panic of that year caused a sudden change of plans, and the show was shipped home to Windsor, by rail to Cleveland, and then driven overland back to the farm.

In the spring of 1874, William Main branched out as an "impresario," with Brown's Concert Company. This concern consisted of just three people, including the manager, who also acted as advance agent and advertiser, using a horse-drawn sulky with saddlebags to carry his bills. The company followed in a buggy and performed wherever they could find a schoolhouse, hotel dining room or even a dancing hall. The totally blind leader, a Mr. Brown, was accompanied by his daughter from Burton, Ohio. Walter put in his first season on the road with this organization. He also spent his vacation term with his father, riding on an improvised seat attached to the axle of the sulky. His duties consisted of distributing bills, advertising the concerts and announcing where the entertainment was to be given. The tour was more or less successful, as the expenses were almost nothing.

The spring of 1875 once more found "Doctor" Main on the road, with his four horses hitched to the bandwagon of Hilliard & Hamilton's forty-horse circus. The show was billed to open at Orwell, Ohio, on May 1, 1875, but strong winds blew the tents down, preventing a performance. The show packed up and drove on to the next stand, Clarindon, and then to Chardon, Ohio, where Walter left the show with his mother to return to the farm for the summer. Young Walter was very disappointed that day because he had great hopes of emulating P.T. Barnum.

In the meantime, Walter resolved to remain at home and show his neighbors that for the next season he could run the 105-acre farm. In true farmer's style, for one season at least, the apparent receipts from a variety of crop goods and products from the farm that season were exactly $300 gross ($7,000 in 2018 dollars). This was extremely little when compared with the show's net profits that amounted to over $100,000 several years later. That same year, Walter was kicked by one of their colts in a playful mood, and this could have been more serious and disfiguring if not for his mother's focused attention.

In 1877, the show started out with Dwight Clapp as the general agent and Walter Main as the assistant agent and billposter boss. This was the first Windsor show or circus to present riding acts and used fifty horses. The show opened in Windsor, Ohio, on May 1 and closed the season at Sigerny (Sigourney), Iowa, that October. Walter rode a pony to the opening and had to sleep in a haystack for lack of any other accommodations.

During the season of 1878, William Main was employed as a boss hostler with Hamilton's & Sargent's New York Circus at a salary of $40 a month and board. Again, Walter retired to the farm with his mother, and as expected, the farming venture failed. The cheese spoiled, the weeds outgrew the corn,

Walter L. Main Circus street parade in Xenia, Ohio. 1892. *Greene County Ohio Historical Society.*

the potatoes rotted in the hill and Walter grew so disgusted with his farming experience that he resolved to abandon the project and establish his own circus. His mother tried to induce him to study law or teach school. But that autumn, Walter traded the cows for horses and farm wagons to start a circus and he formed a partnership with Ephram Burdick and his own father, William Main, who had just finished the season.

Burdick was also a slick horse trader and a close neighbor of the Mains'. They began operations by cutting and making their own stakes, poles and seats. In other words, they built the whole outfit themselves. Burdick furnished the little cash capital required to form this "Great Quadruple Combination." The show opened the season May 10, 1879, at Trumbull Center, Ohio, with four fat plug horses and a new fifty-foot round top. Everything was painted up fresh and fine, but the tent proved too small for the excellent performance presented, which included a wide range of talent and performing animals.

Mrs. Main sold tickets, while Walter was the boss and only property man on the show. The two owners devoted most of their time to horse trading and speculating on the outcome of the season. The outfit was laughed at by the neighbors and was given just a week to start out and end up back home. The show began with an inexperienced general agent named Seth Hill, and the outfit lost money from the start. So Walter was made the official representative and given skillful practical advice by Dwight Clapp on how to be an agent. This, along with a few other changes in the advance, put the circus in the black very quickly.

And contrary to all predictions, the show remained out the entire season and returned with a net profit of $1,000 ($27,000 in 2018 dollars) in cash and a considerable improvement in stock and show property.

At the end of the season, the proprietors returned to Trumbull County for winter quarters. There, William Main sold his half interest to Burdick, who in turn sold that interest to Dan Allen of Ashtabula. Together, they enlarged the show to a twenty-horse outfit. The new circus opened at Ashtabula, Ohio, on May 1, 1880, with

Walter L. Main got a head start in the circus business with his father, William Main. Circa 1895. *Geneva/ Ashtabula County Library.*

Geneva and Rock Creek immediately to follow. Young Walter L. Main was made general agent of this show, and his assistants Charley Chappell and Henry Rich were the lead men of the bill wagon that belonged to Rich. At Bangor, Pennsylvania, in August, Burdick wanted to cut young Main's salary but instead left the show and headed to New York.

Walter consulted with his father and afterwards formed a partnership with F.W. Sargent, of Windsor, Ohio, for the season of 1881. The show started out with twenty-two horses pulling a variety of wagons. Walter drew $50 monthly pay and expenses, with only two men as assistants in doing all of the advance work for the show.

The tent that season was an eighty-foot round top with a small dressing room and no sideshow. The horses were kept in local livery stables, and the staff was fed and lodged at hotels. The 1881 season of the William Main & Company Circus was very pleasant and profitable, from the opening at Orwell, Ohio, to the closing at Brookville, Pennsylvania, on October 1. Sargent was the treasurer, William Main the door tender and Mrs. Main was in charge of the stands and auditor of the books. The performers were the DeAlma family, Pettit and White, Albert Denneier, Kelly the Irish comedian, Winfield's dogs, Dick Vino, Jack Russell, Fred Sylvester and Charley Diamond, the famous harpist and dancer. Frank Griswold was the boss canvas man, who built his own high-quality canvas, including both horse and cooking tents. At the finish of the season, Main bought Sargent's interest, and after the books were balanced, the big show had cleared a net profit of just $5,000 ($130,000 in 2018 dollars). Walter referred to this time as "the happy days when we were young and poor and contented." The winter of 1881–82 was most enjoyable, as it was the first time the Main family had ever been living on easy street in regards to their standard of living.

In 1882, William Main was the sole proprietor; Walter L. Main, while not of age, was the youngest manager in the business; his mother was treasurer of the show; and Dwight Clapp was the general agent. The show had forty horses, an eighty-foot round top, a sideshow, horse tent and a performance that compared favorably with anything ever presented up to that time. The season opened with snow on the ground at Trumbull and moved on to Geneva, then toward Pittsburgh and eastward to New Jersey, Connecticut, Rhode Island, Massachusetts and New York. The show closed the season in New York and wintered on the fairgrounds at Oneonta, New York. To pay for their room and board, the baggage horses were farmed out to work in the lumber woods and a sawmill during the winter. The season of 1882 was a grand success

Main Circus calliope in street parade at Black River Falls, Wisconsin. 1899. *Geneva/Ashtabula County Library.*

for the William Main International Circus. One exception was that Clapp's health failed in the middle of the season, so he had to resign, and Walter took charge of the advance. The touring season was a true pleasure, and at the close Walter and his mother returned to Trumbull for the winter while his father remained with the show at winter quarters.

In 1883, William Main joined hands with M.M. Hilliard, of Orwell, Ohio, to combine their two shows with 114 horses and mules, a menagerie of one elephant, two camels and several cages of wild animals. The owners were equal partners, except in the matter of the elephant, and Walter's services as the general agent were placed against the elephant as an offset. George Castello, one of the most experienced men of the day, was engaged as an instructor for Walter in the matter of laying out routes and advertising, but his services did not prove satisfactory and he was dispensed with before the season was over. To replace him, Dwight Clapp was re-engaged as an assistant and local contractor for the balance of the season. Among the performers that year were William Aymar, Ed Billings, Fred Runnels, the O'Brien Brothers, Hilliard's famous trick horse White Hawk, Babe, the performing elephant, and Walter Main's trick horses and ponies. The Main horses were all trained by Elwood Hamilton, who educated Sir Henry, one of the most versatile and renowned horses of his day. A monument erected to his memory now stands at Windsor Mills, Ohio. The Hilliard and Main Circus opened on April 28, 1883; it closed on December 1 and went into winter quarters at Chetopa, Kansas.

During the season, matters got complicated, and trouble began when Hilliard took a large portion of money to which he was not entitled and left his partner, William Main, to look out for many of the obligations that were incurred at home in wintering and promoting the show.

A number of routing oversights were also discovered that could place the show in the path of the light-fingered gentry and pickpockets, and where the open games of chance and gambling could be run. This necessitated numerous changes in the routing and working arrangements for the balance of the season. But that still didn't prevent a number of illicit gamers from tagging along. It took many years to re-adjust affairs and again get the show sailing in clear waters.

The next spring, a one-third interest was sold to Harry Mack and Giles Pullman, with Pullman as the general agent of the show. The Hilliard, Pullman, and Mack opened at Chetopa, Kansas, in May 1884, and this proved to be the first losing season in the history of the Main show. Walter was made contracting agent in advance and the elder Main was left to the tender mercies of his partners. Conditions became unbearable, and at the end of the season, Walter resigned and returned home to look after his own affairs and determine his next move. The equipment on this show went out on the Pullman, Mack and Company Circus.

In the spring of 1885, Walter, at age twenty-three, started an "Uncle Tom Show" that was a theatrical adaptation of Ohio resident Harriet Beecher Stowe's best seller. The show was staged with wagons, with six horses and two bloodhounds, using cash capital of $800 ($22,000 in 2018 dollars) to start the organization. After a few weeks, he sold the entire outfit to his friend C.G. Phillips, who continued the business with great success. C.G. Phillips operated out of Cortland, Ohio, and had possibly the largest Uncle Tom's Cabin Show of all time. He featured a very fine street parade that included "gabled" cages.

During this interval in 1885, William Main was in Chetopa, Kansas, and was persuaded to sell his interest in the Hilliard. The money he received was very little for his effort, so he left without any real means except three private horses. Main was riding one horse and leading two back to his home in Ohio, making his way as best he could. He reached home just in time to join the first show Walter ever owned outright, but the show was named William Main and Company.

It consisted of four cheap horses, two wagons and a carryall, to which the three performing horses and ponies were added, making a total of seven all told. A tent maker from Boston named Martin trusted Walter for a tent and accepted his notes for the equipment. Fortunately, the entire cash investment did not exceed $600 ($16,500 in 2018 dollars). The show opened in Wellington, Ohio, at the first autumn fair in August and following at other fairs, closed at Canfield, Ohio, in October. The net profit was $200 ($5,500 in 2018 dollars) for two months' work, and they drove back home quite encouraged by their success.

The real feature of this show was the famous Commodore Perry, who was engaged to make up and appear as the "Wild Man of Borneo." His performance was exceptional and to the satisfaction of his friends who were delighted with the humorous action and talent of the "Commodore," who was considered the real comedian of that locality. The most profitable business took place in Ashtabula, Ohio, where the local eccentric "Commodore" was very well known for his antics. There, the citizenry was eager to see the local favorite in his wonderful makeup do his comedy stunts as the wild man. He would do his idea of a war dance and grind his teeth in the height of his frenzy before the audience. The Burton, Ohio, and Conneautville, Pennsylvania engagements were also profitable, as the "Commodore" was well known in those counties and his reputation as a "village cut-up" had extended to that part of the neighboring state as well.

After her husband's departure, Mrs. Main was trying to collect the notes given by the former show for the property as they became due. The proprietors failed to send any money to the Geneva banks as they had promised to do. So as soon as she was able to collect on debts due, she immediately sent the money forward and canceled all of her husband's obligations. When she got through retiring the debts, there was nothing left from the financial wreck of the former show. During this distressing period, the clever and courageous Mrs. Main made and paid most of her expenses by selling corsets and ladies underwear. She often walked from town to town to put in time selling her goods or stopping at the farmhouses both to rest and initiate a sale. She arrived back home, and there was a happy reunion of the Main family.

After consultation, it was decided that Mrs. Main would back Walter for a circus of his own in 1886. So she immediately mortgaged the farm, which was left to her by her father, to raise $1,000 as investment capital. The first winter quarters, an old cheese factory, was purchased for $300, which was paid for by a note, and the building commenced. Fourteen new horses were acquired for the show. This gave the show twenty-one horses. It opened in

Geneva, Ohio, on April 30, 1886, under the title "Walter L. Main's Circus," and closed at Rock Creek, on October 9, with forty horses, all debts paid, and $5,100 ($141,000 in 2018 dollars) in Post Office currency.

Doctor William Main started a show on his own account the following spring (1887), taking in as partners F.W. Sargent and Dwight D. Clapp. After meeting his financial losses, Clapp retired at the end of the season. He took some horses for his interest in the show. William Main and Sargent struggled along for three years until the show was worn out and they had to quit. All the years, the show was titled "William Main and Company Circus."

In 1887, Walter reorganized the Walter L. Main show with forty horses. His mother helped cast new featured performers with Walter. The show opened in Geneva on April 28 and closed in Kinzua, Pennsylvania, on October 19 with all debts paid and a balance of $10,000 ($277,000 in 2018 dollars) in the treasury.

In 1888, the show started as a sixty-horse wagon show. It opened in Geneva on April 28, and closed at Green Back, New York, on October 20 with a net profit of $12,000 ($332,000 in 2018 dollars). This was the first season the Walter L. Main show ever had an elephant, which was rented from Adam Forepaugh for $500 ($14,000 in 2018 dollars) for the season, and the note given for that amount, payable August 1, was promptly paid at maturity. On closing day, everything that was deteriorating or not in first-class condition was sold at auction, and the balance was shipped to Geneva. Among the discarded animals was a pair of lions, one of which was subject to fits due to overfeeding. Also, a broken-down, blind draft horse fell under the auctioneer's gavel to the highest bidder.

It should be noted that from time to time various performers were added to the list of employees already mentioned. Among them were such people as Caster and Carriea, Gorman and Webb, Curley Potts, Jack Russell, Durand and Regan, the DeAlma family and Clark Daugherty, who was the bandmaster. John and Charley Sparks were also part of the show, and the following year John went into business for himself and established John H. Sparks Circus. Also around the show in 1888 were the acts of William Harbeck, Dot Pullman and her partner, Joe Berris, Pop Quinett and family, the Gregory Brothers, Delia Gregory, George Bickle and George S. Cole, the old, experienced showman.

On New Year's Day in 1889, Walter Main, at age twenty-six, purchased all-new horses in Chicago. While in Chicago, changes were in full bloom at the winter quarters in Geneva, where a practically new show was organized, complete with animals rented from Adam Forepaugh. Walter's word and good credit enabled him to start out with a seventy-horse show, but he closed the season with ninety. This was the first season with a regular parade and a real comprehensive circus in all venues. The layout consisted of a 110-foot round-top big top, a 60-foot top sideshow and dressing room, open tent and "push-pole" horse tents, making it the biggest wagon show of its time. The season closed well in the black ink with a net profit of $25,000 ($692,000 in 2018 dollars) with admission at $0.25. That year, all the reserve funds were placed in the banks for safekeeping, and it made a nice tidy sum, but not visible to the naked eye like the post office orders. The 1889 season opened on April 28 at Geneva and closed on October 10 at Somerville, Massachusetts, from where the show was shipped home. The tour covered Pennsylvania and most of New England, with ten weeks in the state of Maine, where the show became "The Main Show" and established a good reputation. In many of these towns with no available railway access, people had not seen an elephant for fourteen years, if ever. Business was to capacity most of the time and the performance applauded to the echo daily.

In 1890 the show was titled "Walter L. Main and Van Amburgh Circus." Hyatt Frost, who owned the Van Amburgh name, did not die until 1895, and it is all but certain that Main leased the title directly from him. The show shipped to Pittsburgh for its first stand and opened on the south side on April 19, giving three shows. It closed in Geneva on October 23 with a profit of $17,000 ($471,000 in 2018 dollars). The show had 120 horses and ten cages of animals, but it was still a wagon show. After the 1890 season, the wagon show equipment was sold to the Scribner & Smith Circus. Scribner had been with the Main Circus in 1889 as the sideshow manager.

The 1891 season was the first time the show was to travel by railroad. The show started with eleven and ended with thirteen railcars. This, of course, increased the expenses, but the circus showed a net profit of $32,000 ($886,000 in 2018 dollars). The season opened at Geneva and closed at Havre de Grace, Maryland, on October 24. The show was shipped back home to Geneva, Ohio, and was housed in the old skating rink, which had been purchased during the summer and was located just opposite the LS&NS Railway Station. It was a conspicuous object of interest for all tourists passing through the city. The horses were always wintered on the Main group of farms at Trumbull, Ohio, about seven miles from Geneva.

The first season by rails was a pleasant experiment, and Walter planned to continue that mode of transportation and build up the show along those lines. The Forepaugh animals had been leased for that season, but in the meantime, Forepaugh had died and the show was sold to P.T. Barnum, James

Animals being unloaded for the Walter L. Main Fashion Plate Show. 1900. *Geneva/Ashtabula County Library.*

A. Bailey and James E. Cooper, who insisted that Main either purchase or return the animals. Bailey insisted that Main pay cash to close the deal on time, and he did. Bailey was so pleased with the transaction that he sold and leased a variety of other animals to Walter.

In 1892, the show started with sixteen railcars with the show and two in advance. George W. Aiken was the general agent that season through 1894. He proved a very efficient man in many respects. Walter Fisher was the contracting agent; Oliver Scott was manager of advertising car no. 1 and Perry Cooke, manager of car no. 2. Frank Train was the circus treasurer during the 1891–93 seasons, and Hugh Harrison was manager of the sideshow from 1891 until 1901. He was associated with the Forepaugh Sells show after leaving the Walter L. Main show.

The season of 1892 opened at Geneva on April 23 and closed at Paragould, Arkansas, on November 19. The show was shipped home and arrived in Geneva, Ohio, just in time for a Thanksgiving dinner. The new acts were the four Walton Brothers, Charles W. Fish, Joe Cousina, Fisher Brothers and a number of others. That season was the first year the show used two rings and a stage. Another elephant, Lizzie, was purchased from George S. Cole for $3,000 ($83,000 in 2018 dollars) on a note. Main also purchased a ticket wagon and some other animals from Cole, and a few animals were acquired from the Cincinnati Zoo. The show had a very impressive menagerie. The season was profitable, but not as much as the previous year.

The 1893 season opened in Geneva on April 22 in a snowstorm. The show traveled on seventeen railcars, fifteen with the show and two in advance. The flat and stock cars were all 60 feet long, and the sleepers were 70 feet in length. The menagerie had two elephants, three camels, an ox and other lead animals. The big top consisted of a 140-foot big top and three 50-foot poles in the center. The menagerie had a 60-foot end with five 30-foot poles in the center and the dressing tent was 50 feet with one 30-foot pole. The cook tent and horse tent were 60 feet with two 30-foot poles in the center.

New on the management staff in 1893 were E.D. Colvin, assistant manager, Charles Bolus, boss canvas man and "Dutch" Rice, who was in charge of tickets. The new talented performers were Mrs. James Stow, Stirk and Zeno, Alexander Seabert and wife, Parrell and Mareno, J.A. Barton as Colvin's assistant, Jim Rane, Judge Palmer and Annie Sylvester.

Everything was going along quite well and business was limited only by the capacity of the tents until the fateful morning of Decoration Day, May 30, 1893. Proceeding with more than customary precaution, the circus train, loaded with its animate and inanimate freight, started gradually down the grade over the hills into Tyrone, Pennsylvania, where the show was to exhibit the next day. The massive train glided down the steep incline with breaks engaged. But, for some unaccountable reason, the train got beyond the control of the engineer and train crew and kept speeding downhill. Rocking and reeling in its mad course, sweeping around the curves, swaying on the steel rails made slippery by the morning dew, the train struck an abrupt curve and toppled over like a house of cards. The heavily laden cars were thrown off the track on their sides and ground both human and animal lives into a gruesome mass of horrible and unsightly forms.

A more detailed description of this terrible calamity is covered in chapter 7, which looks at a well-written report of the scene by an eyewitness. What the records describe shows that the destruction stood unparalleled in railroad history up to that time.

After the wreck, the show remained at Tyrone for eight days while repairs were being made at Altoona, Pennsylvania. Repair work that was feasible, given the limited local resources, was begun at Tyrone. New horses were purchased in Philadelphia because only four out of the wreck were able to work. The citizens of Tyrone helped to load the wagons onto the flatcars.

The Main Circus wreck at Tyrone, with the rail flats, wagon and tableaux a complete shambles. 1893. *Tyrone-Snyder Public Library.*

If Walter Main followed his own inclinations and judgment, he would not have tried to reorganize and continue the season. He initially felt the disaster was so comprehensive that to continue looked hopeless, but all of the performers and other employees were so earnest in their pleadings to go on and not leave them stranded so early in the season, that Main was persuaded to continue. He made repairs and additions as he proceeded along under all sorts of handicaps. The show closed the season at Conneaut, Ohio, on October 14, but no performance was given on that day because of high water, and the show was shipped back to winter quarters. By this time, the show had a new brick building, formerly occupied as a foundry, but better adapted and larger than the old skating rink, which the show had outgrown.

During the winter, the show was practically rebuilt, and it opened the season of 1894 at Geneva on April 21 and closed at Greeneville, Alabama, on December 5. This was the first southern trip for the show, and it was highly successful. It was decided to winter the show at Louisville, Kentucky, instead of returning to Geneva. It went into quarters with eighteen railcars with the show and two in advance, making a total of twenty cars. After deliberation, it was determined to make the show for the season of 1895 one of the best, if not the biggest, on the road. To that end, a loan was negotiated with W.E. Franklin, who was appointed general agent with his own selection of the advance staff and permission to route the show.

The season of 1895 opened in Louisville, Kentucky, on April 15 and was a sight to behold. When the show was erected on the lot, it was outfitted to perfection, with no expenses spared in every detail of the equipment, including the wagons, cages, tableaux, harnesses, flags, banners and plumes. The tents were also new, having been ordered by Main from Chicago, and when erected they fit like a glove. Thus the tenth annual season of the show opened with a parade, which was really a street spectacle on review and was admired by a throng that filled the thoroughfares from curbstones to house tops in the "Gate City" of the sunny South. At the opening, the tents were packed to capacity, and the program, which was an extensive one, passed off without a flaw or mishap, so careful had been the rehearsals under the direction of Fred W. Aymar, the equestrian manager. After the auspicious opening, the show continued on the route with such triumphs and success that it was able to meet all obligations and pay off the loan. The show continued on, with varied success touring Texas and the South and closing the season at Glasgow, Kentucky, on November 16, and was shipped directly to Geneva, Ohio, for the winter.

The 1897 season opened at Ashtabula, Ohio, on April 17, in a snowstorm and continued along the lake towns to Toledo, Ohio, where it was still cold, and then proceeded to Indiana, Illinois, Missouri, Kansas, Colorado, Utah, Idaho, Oregon, Washington and for three days by boat to Vancouver, British Columbia. The show returned to the United States and on July 26 played Portland, Oregon, where it was found necessary to make some material changes in the advance management before starting on the coast trip over the Southern Pacific railway to California and into the southwest. The show closed the season at Rolla, Missouri, on November 6 and was then shipped home to Geneva.

On such an extensive trip, it should be mentioned how easy it is to make mistakes and to be misled by placing too much confidence in those whose reputation had not stood the test of time and reliability. Main, the previous season, was induced to secure the services of Dan Vernon, a man who was reputed to know the western country from end to end and had often visited that section with the John Robinson show. He was dispatched to the coast to inspect and look over the country to get rates from the railways and make reports as he made progress. This he failed to do, and the omission was not discovered until the next season when the show reached the southwestern territory, approaching it from the east.

The first error was encountered in Colorado, where it became necessary to transfer to a narrow-gauge railway to make some of the side trips to towns that had almost entirely disappeared since Vernon had visited them in years gone by. No special provisions had been made for a change from their own broad-gauge cars while on this side journey. The delays were hard, and the business was worse. The circus showed a loss of over $1,000 ($30,000 in 2018 dollars) a day while in this region. An investigation proved Vernon had not scouted that territory at all and knew nothing about the conditions as they existed at that time. The result was maddening, and it was then discovered that Vernon made some of the contracts with the western railroads without notifying his employer the season before. These contracts could not be changed without a great deal of expense. The same conditions prevailed in the far northwest and up into British Columbia, which he had not visited at all until it was about time for the advance force to reach that point. The season, so far, had many ups and downs, and business was universally bad. The weather also proved unusually out of season, and the third advertising car was cut off to save expenses. Upon arrival in Portland, Oregon, a consultation was held and Vernon was dismissed. Clay Lambert was made railway contractor; Ed Knupp, then treasurer, was made general agent, which was his first experience at that line; and Charles Bernard, who was the bookkeeper, was also appointed treasurer. Walter then went to San Francisco to take charge of the advance, which he continued to do for the balance of the season. Strangely enough, with Walter heading advance, the business began to pick up at Portland and ran remarkably well for the balance of the tour, with the San Francisco engagement proving very profitable. As a significant feature, they had the first group of performing wild animals ever in that part of the country with a circus.

In 1898, the show opened in Geneva on April 23 and was to close at Burton, Ohio, on October 22. The dining car was omitted in 1898, leaving nineteen cars with the show train and two in advance. The territory covered was Pennsylvania, New York, Connecticut, Massachusetts, New Hampshire, Maine, Vermont, Maryland, West Virginia and Canada. The season was a success, and a baby elephant arrived by purchase with its foster mother, who took care of the little fellow and nursed it with a jealous care. He was christened Admiral Dewey. The show had a big new canvas, new people, and William Sells, who was in his boyhood one of the most graceful riders of his time, as the general agent. He was also the son of Allen Sells, who was one of the famous Sells brothers. The Spanish-American War was on, and the show opened the same day that war was declared. On the closing day, all of the animals and horses were sold to the Orrin Brothers of Mexico City, Mexico, and were shipped to that location.

The season of 1899 was eventful and opened in Geneva on April 29. It began by making another Pacific coast trip, which was very profitable because it was well routed and advertised and made a tremendous hit everywhere. The feature was the great sixty-three horse act in a concentric ring, trained and performed by R.H. Dockrill, the well-known equestrian director, who also had charge of the performance. There were twenty-two railcars with the show and two in advance. Upon arrival in San Francisco, additional people were engaged. The tents were erected at Twelfth and Market Streets, and extra lights were erected. The tents were profusely decorated with flags, banners, flowers, plants and palms, making them look like a tropical garden on a festive holiday. The season and tour proved a great success, and the profits were close to $75,000 ($2.25 million in 2018 dollars). The baby elephant was injured while carelessly being taught some performing tricks back at the winter quarters and unfortunately died from the effects. The trainer most likely never comprehended how very lucky he was that the baby's foster mother was on the road.

In January 1900, Main, who was now thirty-eight years old, was determined to retire from show business, or at least take a long vacation and get much-

Walter L. Main Circus bandwagon with orchestra. Circa 1890. *Geneva/Ashtabula County Library.*

needed rest. So the show was advertised and with the exception of eight cars and their contents, which were leased to Rhoda Royal for a show, everything else was sold at auction. Walter then took his long-promised trip to Europe, where he spent most of the summer. While in Europe, he visited the Barnum & Bailey's Greatest Show on Earth.

On returning home from his splendid vacation, Walter found a payment had been made to his bank in Geneva. The deposit was made by Rhoda Royal and his partners as rent for the show that Walter had not seen but once or twice all season long. The Rhoda Royal management concluded that they could cut down the equipment and reduce the show to four cars, play some of the smaller towns and remain in the South all winter; but again, this experiment was a failure and they went broke on the proposition.

Feeling greatly rejuvenated and fresh from his foreign trip, Walter decided to re-organize and re-fit the show and start out in the spring of 1901 with an entirely new, up-to-date circus, copied somewhat after the show style he witnessed in Europe. Soon after starting, with sixteen cars and one advertising car, it was discovered that the outfit would not do, and ten cages of animals, a drove of camels and six more cars were added.

During the summer, an entirely new winter quarters was built one mile west of Geneva, Ohio, on a new farm adjoining the LS&MS and the Nickel Plate railroad tracks, with switch connections right on the grounds. The show opened in Geneva on May 4, 1901, and its route went through New England and on to Long Island for eleven days, which proved five days too much, and then headed to Vermont, New Hampshire, and south to New Jersey, and then to Baltimore, Washington, and other southern cities. The season closed at Tennille, Georgia, on December 7 and was shipped home.

As usual, the season of 1902 opened in Geneva on April 19 and closed at Roxboro, North Carolina, on November 11. The show was on twenty-five railcars, with two in advance. It had three rings, a stage and the great hippodrome track. This was the first time the show ever played Boston, and it made a tremendous hit in establishing itself as a big show in the New England region, where the Barnum & Bailey and the Adam Forepaugh shows had always been dominant. After Boston, all of the eastern territory was played to a greatly increased business over previous seasons, and as a whole the tour proved highly successful. The new lineup of talented acts that year included the Boise Family, Olga Reed (a granddaughter of old Dan Rice), William Devan, Lizzie Rooney, Blanch Hilliard, Essie Fay, William Melrose and the Martel Family. They made up an exceptionally strong program and presented it in such a manner as to command the attention of the public everywhere.

Main circus show performers and staff pose for a group photo. Circa 1895. *Geneva/Ashtabula County Library.*

In 1903, the show was increased to twenty-nine cars with three advertising cars. The tour opened at Springfield, Ohio, on April 18 and closed at Tazewell, Virginia, on October 31. The circus played Ohio, Pennsylvania, New York, New Hampshire, Maine, Massachusetts, Vermont, New Jersey, Maryland, Washington, D.C., and Canada. The layout was the finest the show had ever used and consisted of a 150-foot big top with four 30-foot center pieces and all other tents in that proportion. There were twenty-five cages, five elephants, eight camels and two hundred horses and ponies, all loaded on one train. The feature that season was a spectacular production of "Savage South Africa" presented with a number of real warriors from the Congo. In Oxford, Pennsylvania, lightning struck one of the stable tents and eighteen fine draft horses were killed. But on the whole, the season was pleasant and profitable, with good weather and practically no opposition.

The executive staff of the 1904 season of the Walter L. Main Shows were Hugh Harrison, manager, Geneva, Ohio; Edward C. Knupp, general agent, Geneva; Dr. C.M. Stull, superintendent of labor, parade and forage, Geneva; John Gill, musical director, Circleville, Ohio; William Elliott, superintendent of refreshments, Evansville, Indiana; Richard Jones, superintendent of menageries, Geneva; James Whalen, superintendent of canvas, Geneva; W.W. Scott, superintendent of stock, Cincinnati, Ohio; Peter Hirtz, master of transportation, Collingdale, Pennsylvania; Henry Pullman, leader of parade and superintendent of annex door, Buffalo, New York; Albert Pancost, in charge of winter quarters, Geneva; and A.J. Trunkey, attorney, of Geneva, Ohio. The season opened in Geneva on April 23 and closed at Charleston, West Virginia, on October 18. The circus played the longest, most crooked route on record. The show went through Pennsylvania, Ohio, New York, Vermont, Michigan, Wisconsin, Minnesota, North Dakota, Montana, Idaho, Wyoming, Nebraska, Iowa, Indiana, West Virginia and Virginia. The pictorial printing alone that year amounted to exactly $26,689.98 ($767,000 in 2018 dollars), which shows that circus business involved a great deal of competition.

For years, Walter L. Main had provided a Christmas Day dinner for the men employed in and around the show's winter quarters at Geneva, Ohio. This fact was known to all the laborers with the show, and many of them made early arrangements to be on hand at the winter reunion. The Christmas of 1904 was no exception, and, in fact, the dinner provided exceeded all

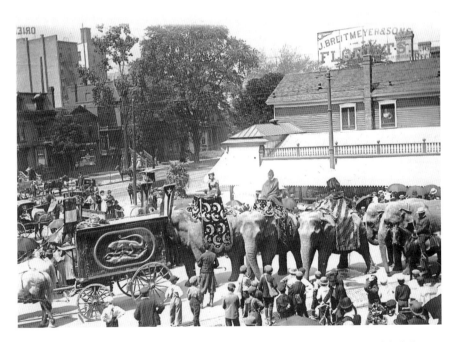

Main circus street parade with a line of adored elephants. Circa 1896. *Geneva/Ashtabula County Library.*

expectations. Approximately one hundred people sat down to the tables in the long dining room at winter quarters and were served turkey, chicken, assorted vegetables, plum pudding and pumpkin pie. Afterwards, everyone adjourned to the reading room, where everyone received as gifts two suits of underwear, two pairs of heavy socks, a pair of rubber boots and mittens. The entertainment was provided by the local village quartette and banjo.

During the winter of 1904–05, everything was fully repaired and placed in good order and the circus portion of his show was sold to William P. Hall. Walter Main remained at home that summer, enjoying himself after seeing his property well placed and earning good money without any effort on his part. However, some trouble with Hall arose through business complications, which were subsequently resolved.

It is a notable fact that whenever Walter Main handled his circus in his own way, under his own management, everything went well. But when he turned it over to others or left it to run itself on the automatic plan, things would often turn disastrous.

Walter Main announced that for reasons of ill health (probably more emotional than physical), he was now selling the menagerie portion and was going out of business. Proprietors or representatives of all the leading circuses and menageries in the country made a special point of attending this particular auction. His subsequent plan was to once again travel abroad.

The auction of course began in Geneva on January 24, 1905, with the sale of harnesses and miscellaneous paraphernalia. The following day, the wild animals were put under the auctioneer's gavel and sold to the highest bidder. Among the leading showmen present at this auction were Lewis Sells, of the Forepaugh & Sells Circus, and a representative of Barnum-Bailey. Also in attendance were John Robinson Jr., of Cincinnati, and one of the Sun brothers. After selling his circus, Walter L. Main stayed well connected to the circus business by renting and leasing equipment to a variety of smaller operations and carnivals.

CHAPTER 5

THE PERFORMERS, ACTS AND CIRCUS SUPPLIERS

T he circuses were advertised using the credibility of the owner's good name. But the billboards had to fully emphasize the skill and talent of the performers in order to draw a crowd. Here are just a few of the many talented Ohio performers that graced the three rings.

ANNIE OAKLEY

Few would argue that probably the most renowned circus performer from Ohio was Annie Oakley (1860–1926), who was born Phoebe Ann Mosey in Darke County, Ohio. This petite, unassuming young lady who had humble beginnings in life would perform for U.S. presidents and European royalty. When Annie was six years old, her father died of pneumonia, leaving her mother with six children and no means of support. Annie's mother remarried, but her second husband died soon after the marriage, leaving her mother with a new infant.

Biographer Shirl Kasper recounted Annie Oakley's own story about how at only eight years old, she took a rifle from the house and fired her very first shot at a squirrel. "I saw a squirrel run down over the grass in front of the house, through the orchard and stop on a fence to get a hickory nut. It was a wonderful shot, going right through the head from side to side."

When Annie was about nine years old, she and her sister Sarah Ellen went to live at the Darke County Infirmary, which housed orphaned children, the elderly and the mentally ill. In exchange for helping with the children, Annie received additional education and learned the skill of sewing from Mrs. Edington, the wife of the infirmary superintendent. Annie would later take advantage of her skill to design and tailor her own costumes. She also endured harsh mental and physical treatment from a family that paid the infirmary to have her "bounded to them" as a domestic helper for several years. She finally ran away and returned home. By the time she was able to rejoin her family, Annie's mother had married a third time. But the family's household earnings were still meager at best. As a result, Annie

Annie Oakley remains an Ohio legend and icon for her expert shooting skills. Circa 1880. *The Greenville Carnegie Library.*

used her father's old Kentucky rifle and hunting skill to supply the Charles & Anthony Katzenberger grocery store in Greenville, Ohio, with small game. The store would act as a supplier to provide hotels and restaurants in Cincinnati with game meat. Annie was so successful at hunting that she was able to pay off the mortgage on her mother's house with the money she earned by the time she was just fifteen years old.

Her renowned marksmanship came to the attention of Jack Frost, a Cincinnati hotel owner who was regularly purchasing Annie's game. And although the exact date was never recorded, it is believed that in 1875 the well-known expert marksman Frank E. Butler (1847–1926) placed a $100 wager ($2,300 in 2018 dollars) with Jack Frost that he could best any local fancy shooter.

Frost accepted the bet and made arrangements for a shooting match on Thanksgiving Day 1875 between Butler and Annie, saying, "The last opponent Butler expected was a five-foot-tall 15-year-old girl named Annie." Frost most likely used Annie's age to intimidate Butler, draw a crowd and gain publicity for himself. Butler lost the match and the wager in the twenty-fifth round of shooting. But he was fascinated by Annie's ability and confidence. He soon began courting Annie, and they were married on

August 23, 1876. There is a recorded certificate of another wedding on June 20, 1882, in Windsor, Ontario. It is possible that their first wedding wasn't properly documented since there are no known records. But given the nature of their devotion for each other, perhaps they just wanted to renew their nuptial covenant now that Annie was in the public eye and twenty-one years old.

For a while, Frank and Annie Butler made Cincinnati their home. In 1881, the Sells Brothers Circus signed the Baughman and Butler team as an expert marksman act and billed them as "Champion Rifle Dead-Shots of the World." But at some point during the season, Baughman left the act and was replaced by John E. Graham. Annie got her big break toward stardom with Sells Brothers the following season, when she had to stand in for John Graham, who fell ill and could not perform. Annie immediately proved to be a crowd-pleaser and then continued as part of the act. She adopted the stage name of Oakley when she and Frank began performing together. In March 1884, just prior to joining Sells Brothers again, Butler and Oakley performed in St. Paul, Minnesota, and in the audience was the famous Native American Sitting Bull, who had been among the leaders in the defeat of eccentric Ohio native Lieutenant Colonel George Armstrong Custer at the Battle of Little Bighorn in 1876. Sitting Bull was so impressed by her skill as a woman that he wanted to meet her and offered $65 ($1,700 in 2018 dollars) for a photograph of the two of them together. During this meeting, Sitting Bull took such a liking to Annie that he "adopted her" by bestowing the name "Watanya Cicilla," or "Little Sure Shot," upon her. Ever the savvy businessman, Butler placed an advertisement in a trade publication talking up the meeting. That same year, the Sells Brothers Circus signed Butler and Oakley as the "Champion Rifle Shots," but they stayed with the circus for just one season.

After wrapping up their 1884 season with Sells Brothers, they joined Buffalo Bill's Wild West Show in 1885. During her first season with the Buffalo Bill show, Oakley was engaged in a competitive rivalry with Lillian Smith, who was also a rifle sharpshooter. Oakley left the Buffalo Bill show, but upon Lillian Smith's departure, she returned in time for the Buffalo Bill show's European tour and the 1889 Paris Exposition.

In Europe, she performed for Queen Victoria of the United Kingdom and other crowned heads of Europe. At his own request, Oakley shot the ashes off a cigarette held in the hand of the newly crowned Kaiser Wilhelm II of Germany. This three-year European tour advanced Oakley's reputation as an American entertainment star. Her earnings during the tour were second only to those of "Buffalo Bill" Cody himself.

Oakley was an advocate for women to be allowed to serve in combat operations for the United States armed forces. She penned a letter to President William McKinley, dated April 5, 1898, offering the government the services of a company of fifty fully qualified "lady sharpshooters" who would provide their own arms and ammunition in the event the United States would declare war with Spain. The Spanish-American War did break out, but Oakley's offer was denied. Theodore Roosevelt did, however, name his group of volunteers the "Rough Riders" after the "Buffalo Bill's Wild West and Congress of Rough Riders of the World," where Annie Oakley was a star performer and headliner.

In October 1901, just a month after president William McKinley was fatally shot by an assassin in Buffalo, New York, Oakley was also badly injured in a train accident in North Carolina. Newspaper articles from that time state that she was thrown out of her berth and severely injured her back. She was only able to recover following five spinal surgeries.

But Annie was drafted back into the national limelight again in 1904, when newspaper mogul William Randolph Hearst published a false story about her. Hearst owned a national media chain that was famous for a lurid style of reporting called "yellow journalism." A Hearst newspaper called the *Chicago American* reported that Annie Oakley had been arrested for stealing to support a cocaine habit. The woman actually arrested was a burlesque performer who told Chicago police that her name was Any Oakley when her name was actually Maude Fontanella.

Most of the newspapers that printed the story had relied on the Hearst article via telegraph wire, and they promptly printed a retraction and an apology upon learning of the libelous error. But Hearst tried to avoid paying an anticipated court judgment of $20,000 (equivalent to $545,000 in 2018) by sending a private investigator to Darke County, Ohio, with orders to obtain reputation-damaging details regarding Oakley's past. The investigator was not able to find anything viable. Oakley then spent the next six years winning fifty-four of fifty-five libel lawsuits against various newspapers. Although she collected a considerable amount in judgment payments, the total proved less than her legal expenses. But when it was all over, Annie's Oakley's reputation was vindicated.

By 1925, Oakley's health began to deteriorate, and she died on November 3, 1926, in Greenville, Ohio, at the age of sixty-six; her ashes were buried at Brock Cemetery near Greenville. She has since been inducted into both the National Women's Hall of Fame and the Ohio Women's Hall of Fame.

CLYDE BEATTY

Circus great and Ohio native Clyde Beatty was a world-renowned animal trainer, movie actor and circus owner. Beatty was born June 10, 1903, in Bainbridge, a small town near Chillicothe, Ohio. The eldest of nine children, he graduated from Chillicothe High School. In August 1921, Beatty climbed aboard a freight train heading to Washington Court House, Ohio, where he found employment by joining the Howes Great London Circus.

Beatty's first job was as a cage boy for the circus's animal trainer Louis Roth and later for John "Chubby" Guilfoyle. He quickly discovered he had a knack for working with and training the large cats and by 1923 began working a small mixed-animal act in the circus.

In 1925, Beatty was working for American Circus Corporation's Hagenbeck-Wallace Circus when the show's featured animal trainer, Pete Taylor, fell ill and young Beatty was asked to take over the act. Taylor's act consisted of twenty-five lions and tigers, a huge challenge for someone who was still a novice animal trainer. This is when Beatty, who was a true showman, began developing his own unique style of the "fighting animal act" performance.

He would quickly enter the steel bar arena cage with his safari pith helmet, whip, cane-bottom chair and a pistol loaded with blank cartages. This breathtaking, fast-paced and exciting style became an overnight success as it kept the audience members on the edge of their seats. Following the 1929 purchase of the American Circus Corporation by John N. Ringling, which included the Hagenbeck-Wallace Circus, his nephew John Ringling North could see great potential in Beatty as a star attraction. From 1931 until 1934, John Ringling North featured Beatty's performance on the opening dates of the Ringling Bros. and Barnum & Bailey Circus in New York City and Boston. In 1932, Beatty was critically injured and was close to death after being mauled by a lion. Beatty had become such a drawing card for the circus that John Ringling North postponed the New York City opening to afford Beatty more time to recover from his injuries.

Clyde Beatty was now an American circus icon. Many circuses wanted the Beatty act because the use of his name on circus ad posters meant substantial earnings. On September 13, 1933, while showing in Bristol, Tennessee, Clyde and circus aerialist Harriett Evans slipped away from the show just long enough to get married. In 1935, Clyde Beatty performed for the Cole Brothers Circus, which was owned by Jess Adkins and Zack

Terrell. Then, in 1943, he performed for Art Concello in the Clyde Beatty–Russell Brothers Circus.

During the winter of 1944–45, Beatty purchased the Wallace Brothers Circus, which was a truck show, and in April 1945 the Clyde Beatty Circus premiered. The show did so well its first season that Beatty decided to sell his "truck show" equipment to Floyd King and purchased part interest in Art Concello's fifteen-railcar show, the Russell Brothers Pan Pacific Circus. This then became the Clyde Beatty Circus, and in 1947 Beatty became the sole owner of the show. The circus was a large tented circus with a big menagerie and was a beautiful sight on the lot. The circus showed mostly in western states, usually opening in Southern California.

During the 1950s, at least two movies were filmed on the show—*Ring of Fear*, starring Clyde Beatty, Mickey Spillane and Pat O'Brien, and also *Three Ring Circus*, starring Dean Martin, Jerry Lewis and Zsa Zsa Gabor.

Between 1950 and 1952, a syndicated radio series, *The Clyde Beatty Show*, was on the air. The show was a weekly adventure series loosely based on Beatty's career. Actually, Beatty was never on the show because the voice of a radio actor was used as a stand-in.

In March 1956, the circus opened in Burbank, California. Movie actor Duncan Renaldo (the Cisco Kid) had been added to the show as a star attraction. The season's business was bad from the start and did not improve. On May 9, the Clyde Beatty Circus folded and returned to quarters.

Frank McClosky and Walter Kernan stepped in and paid the lien on the Beatty circus. Then they reopened the show on August 29 in New Mexico and completed the remainder of the season. At the close of the season, McClosky and Kernan moved the circus to Deland, Florida, where they began using the site of the old Johnny J. Jones Show (a railroad carnival) as their winter headquarters.

The year 1956 was a bad financial season for circuses. Even Ringling Bros. and Barnum & Bailey Circus had to close mid-season and restructure to cut costs and began showing just in arenas and stadiums starting in 1957. The Clyde Beatty Circus ended that same year in near bankruptcy. After paying off the additional liens, Frank McClosky, Walter Kernan, Jerry Collins and Randolph Calhoun, who had formed the Acme Circus Operating Corporation, stepped in and renamed the show the Clyde Beatty Cole Bros. Circus for the 1958 season, and Beatty continued to perform his wild animal act.

In 1964, Beatty was diagnosed with cancer. He continued to perform until his health and strength no longer permitted. Beatty opened the season in

1965 but soon had to retire to his home in Ventura, California, where he died on July 19, 1965.

There were many other great performers and acts that contracted with the various high-profile circuses. Here are just a few of the extremely talented nineteenth-century circus performers.

WILLIAM BADGER

For many years a black man with a white mustache cared for the Sells Brothers Circus elephants. His name was Bill Badger, and he was called "Old Badger." Badger had been with the Sells Circus since the late 1880s and was listed in the Sells route books as William Badger, head elephant man. Badger was later with the M.L. Clark Circus, traveling in charge of their elephants. It is believed that Badger died sometime around 1915.

WILLIAM E. BURKE

William E. Burke (1845–1906) was a fabulous clown who sang comic songs and tumbled. This Ohio native may be forgotten, but his daughter was Billie Burke, the actress who plays the role of Glenda the Good Witch in the 1939 MGM classic *The Wizard of Oz*. A press agent, Charles Day, described him as a happy-go-lucky, genial individual. Born in Knox County, Ohio, his father arranged for him to become a druggist apprentice in Fredericktown, Ohio and later he became a dry goods clerk in Pittsburgh. During the Civil War, he joined the Union army at age sixteen and was involved in six major battles. During his enlistment, he was very popular because of his comical songs and jokes about the daily life of a soldier. He was later seriously injured and given an honorable discharge. After the war, he was engaged for a short stint with a minstrel troupe and then joined the James M. Nixon circus company, which after a brief southern tour set sail for Galveston, Texas. The ship ran into severe weather and was nearly destroyed. Burke was picked up by an American steamship and set ashore in New Orleans. There, he joined Thayer and Noyes playing up the Red River on the steamer *Ida May*. Once again, a storm wrecked his vessel, but Burke survived, having only lost his personal effects and wardrobe. He played with top circuses such as Thayer

& Noyes Circus, Adam Forepaugh and Barnum, Bailey & Hutchinson. He was with the Sells Brothers circus for the 1885–86 seasons. During that time, he was billed: "Billy Burke, of the Sells Brothers Shows, is an old soldier, but none of his jokes are." Burke was one of the greatest vocal jesters of the big top tent world and at age sixty-one died in England.

BILLY CARROLL

Billy Carroll had a spectacular comedy clown show in the late nineteenth century and was often the headliner on circus billboards and posters. Starting in 1893, Billy transformed his clown act into a unique show. As part of the colorful seven-scene presentation, Billy was assisted by his brother, who received no billing at all. The performance of these two white-faced clowns was either connected to a small traveling show or attached to a larger, full-scale circus, such as the Sells Brothers Show.

WILD MEN OF BORNEO

During the latter half of the nineteenth century, there was a popular sideshow touring act known as the Wild Men of Borneo. But this was a contrived hoax, because the Davis Brothers, Hiram and Barney Davis, were not in any way natives of Borneo. The elder brother, Hiram, was born in England in 1825, and Barney in 1827 in New York. The brothers were dwarves who stood approximately three feet, seven inches tall. Their parents eventually settled in Knox County, Ohio, where they were raised on a farm.

In 1852, the brothers started their exhibition career when Lyman Warner, a show promoter, purchased the brothers from their mother, who was widowed and financially completely destitute. Warner then created an intriguing personality for the two brothers and renamed them Waino and Plutano. They were promoted as heathen savages from the dark Asian island of Borneo. The general public knew very little about the island of Borneo, and the area was still veiled in mystery. For this reason, the public bought into the story in its entirety. The brothers fully played up their roles, and during exhibitions the "Wild Men" pretended to be wild and spoke an unintelligible language and in time developed characters. Waino was portrayed as a gentle savage who read poems, while Plutano was a stubborn, ornery character. Both brothers possessed extraordinary strength given their size and would periodically lift audience volunteers off their feet.

Lyman Warner passed away in 1871, and his son Hanford took over managing the brothers' careers. By 1882, Waino and Plutano became involved with P.T. Barnum and his traveling exhibitions. With Barnum's fabled promotional skill, their fame and the careers of the Wild Men of Borneo escalated. Over the next twenty-five years of their career, the brothers earned an average of $8,000 a year ($220,000 in 2018 dollars), or nearly $200,000 ($5.5 million in 2018 dollars), which was an enormous amount of money at that time.

The Davis brothers both retired in 1903. In 1905, Hiram (Waino) died of natural causes. Seven years later, in March 1912, Barney (Plutano) joined his brother at the advanced age of eighty-five. The brothers are buried side by side at their boyhood home of Mount Vernon, Ohio.

THE OHIO CIRCUS SUPPLIERS

During the many years of the demand for first-class equipment, costumes, printing and other supplies by the Robinson, Sells and other shows, various business enterprises that invested heavily in real estate, buildings and facilities to supply the wants and needs of the entire amusement industry were established in Cincinnati. Some of the finest lithographed and engraved paper ever produced was manufactured by several plants that operated a large number of years. Railcars, tents, wagons, carved chariots, bandwagons, animal dens, steam calliopes, uniforms, costumes, showboats, cars and numerous articles were being produced in the city.

Barnum's partner W.C. Coup was the innovator who first put a very big, full-scale circus on the rails in 1872. But this is a legend started by Coup, who was also a classic self-promoter. He was once quoted as stating that he was the first circus owner to make practical use of railroad cars and locomotives.

Although Coup was not the first showman to use railroad technology to transport his show, he was by far an innovator and manager who implemented drastically needed efficient ways of loading wagons and materials that ushered in a new era of circus business and management.

W.C. Coup and Dan Castello devised a system to load circus wagons onto flatcars using ramps and bridge plates between railcars. They also employed a system of ropes, pulleys and a winch stand to get the wagons onto and off of the flatcars. Horses pulled the wagons up the ramp, and a second team would pull the wagons down the flatcars. Off-loading was much the same as loading, but a winch stand was used to help brake a wagon during its descent down the ramp. First used in 1872, the system is still used today.

As circuses moved to travel by train, they began by using flatcars from the Pennsylvania Railroad, which turned out to be hazardous because the Pennsylvania Railroad's cars were not in the best condition for the specific needs of a circus. Coup had railcar manufacturer John L. Gill, of Columbus, Ohio, fabricate special flatcars made to his specifications. After Coup took delivery of the special flatcars, the P.T. Barnum Circus departed Columbus made up of sixty cars, including flatcars carrying about one hundred show wagons. Although many accidents have occurred during the decades, circus rail travel has proved to be well suited for transporting heavy equipment required to outfit a circus, in addition to performers and animals. John L. Gill & Company also manufactured flat transport railcars for the Sells Brothers Circus's 1878 season.

As early as 1867, circus wagons began being fabricated in Cincinnati, and one specific order that year was filled for Dan Castello. It is believed that the builder may have been Henry Ohlsen Sr., who opened his doors in 1864, the first year for many Queen City circus wagon manufacturers such as George Schmidt and others. One carriage builder named Louis Havekotte was Ohlsen's partner from the start of the firm until 1875, when the firm went bankrupt. It should be mentioned that Ohlsen gained fame for his special ability to construct unique steam calliope wagons.

Striking out on his own, Havekotte entered into partnership with William Bode (1835–1914) in 1878. Three years later, they had constructed several parade wagons for the John Robinson circus. Bode sold his interest to Charles Puhlman in May 1885 and proceeded to established a wagon and plow manufacturing shop in his own name at the northwest corner of Livingston Road and Central Avenue in Cincinnati.

William's son Albert Bode (1869–1928) was made general manager of the business sometime prior to 1902. Albert Bode expanded the business by turning out massive baggage, cage and parade wagons for both large and small circus operators. The Bode wagons were railroad show vehicles, built stronger than those of the 1890s and the previous decade. These wagons were constructed to carry heavier loads to minimize the number of wagons and consequent train length. The wagons were basically large boxes, modified as required, with bars in the sides for cages, or carvings secured

ESTIMATES GIVEN ON REPAIRING AND PAINTING WAGONS AND AUTOMOBILES.

THE BODE WAGON CO.

MANUFACTURERS OF
ALL KINDS OF

CUSTOM MADE WAGONS

BODE

THE CINCINNATI FIRM
WITH A
NATIONAL REPUTATION.

TELEPHONE WEST 2834

OFFICE:
1649-1673 CENTRAL AVE

CINCINNATI, O., Feb. 14, 1928.

Bode Wagon Company advertising signage. Bode was one of several premier circus wagon fabricators, along with Sullivan & Eagle, operating out of Cincinnati. 1928. *Cincinnati & Hamilton County Library.*

to the sides for parade vehicles. The wheel diameters were reduced since they would no longer encounter rutted country roads as did overland show vehicles. However, wet circus grounds required the contact area between the wheel and the ground be increased to support the wagon's great weight, and so the tire widths were increased.

Over the years, Bode produced some of the most ornately designed tableau wagons of the very early 1900s. But as World War I approached, business began to drop off sharply.

Bode's last large order came in 1917, when he was selected to supply and mount the truck bodies for Frank J. Spellman's ill-fated U.S. Motorized Circus. The order was well suited to Bode, who was in the process of retooling his product line from wagons to custom truck bodies. There was just enough ceiling clearance in the Bode shop for workmen to assemble the Spellman tableau bodies.

The Spellman wagon bodies represented a style of wagon different from the previous wagons Bode built. Many incorporated an abundance of furniture and architectural-styled moldings, scrollwork and painting, and less in the way of carved figures. Generally, the carvings were simpler in execution but still presented an impressive array of workmanship. The bodies were mounted on a chassis by Kelly Motor Truck Company of Springfield, Ohio.

However, as was typical of most newly launched circuses, Spellman's was severely underfinanced and was put out of business as quickly as it started. The circus only performed three days, with two of those days being in Columbus, the capital city.

P.J. Hart was a staff mechanic for Kelly Motor assigned to go on the road with the trucks. Hart had delivered a check to Bode for $75,000 to pay for the truck bodies prior to their release. As a result, Kelly Motor Truck Co. ended up owning the Bode bodies instead of Spellman or Bode. Since Kelly Motor had no use for circus bodies, they sold them to various circuses, and they were converted back to parade wagons. Some of the bodies went to carnivals that converted them into show fronts.

Cincinnati, Ohio, was home to several great show-printing establishments. The W.H. Donaldson Company began publishing the *Billboard*, which is America's most outstanding and comprehensive circus trade periodical. *Billboard* was started as a trade journal for the billboard posting industry in 1894, and it carried some circus news because circuses were prominent in the use of billboards. Soon, the focus shifted to an emphasis on circuses, carnivals and other venues of amusement. Other Cincinnati printing establishments include the Gibson & Company, the Krebs Lithographing Company and

After James A. Bailey acquired a one-third interest in the Sells Brothers Circus, he used the names of Adam Forepaugh and Peter, Ephraim and Lewis Sells to form a combined circus show that premiered in 1896. Circa 1896. Printer: The Strobridge Lithographing Company. *Cincinnati Art Museum.*

the Enquirer Job Printing Company. Three circus poster print houses that produced truly fine art products that are still valuable today are Donaldson Lithograph, Russell-Morgan and Strobridge & Co. Lithographers.

In January 1867, John F. Robinson Jr. and James M. Armstrong financed and formed a partnership with printers A.O. Russell and Robert J. Morgan. They acquired the Enquirer Job Printing Rooms, which had previously been the printing division of the *Cincinnati Enquirer*. The printing rooms occupied the first and second stories of the building at 20 College Street in downtown Cincinnati, Ohio. The firm started out producing theatrical and circus posters, labels and placards. Within five years, business had increased so much that in November 1872, the business relocated into a new four-story building.

In 1880, Russell convinced his partners to expand into producing playing cards. The partners concurred, and two additional stories were added to their building, making it a six-story facility. Customized printing equipment was designed and built to meet Russell-Morgan & Company's specifications. On June 28, 1881, the company turned out its first deck of playing cards and continued to manufacture approximately 1,600 packs a day. In 1891, Russell, Morgan and Company changed its name to the United States Printing Company and in 1901 became the United States Lithograph Co.

The Strobridge Lithographing Company was incorporated in 1867. The company was originally established in 1847 by a Cincinnati engraver named Elijah J. Middleton. In 1854. Middleton decided to form a partnership with a lithographer, W.R. Wallace, and local book vendor Hines Strobridge. But at the end of the Civil War, Strobridge bought out the partners and renamed the company. Beginning in the 1880s, as the Strobridge firm specialized in poster printing, it established offices in New York and London, with a representative in Sydney. In 1887, the company's production shop was completely destroyed by fire. Strobridge wasted no time relocating and rebuilding on Canal Street and increased both its national and international sales. An 1896 advertisement made a point of stating, "You see Strobridge posters all Over the World." It produced circus posters for the Sells Brothers, Adam Forepaugh, James Bailey, the Ringling Brothers and many others. Well into the twentieth century, Strobridge produced posters for the motion picture industry. Hines Strobridge's lithograph firm was purchased in 1960 and remained open until 1971, when it closed its doors.

The Barney & Smith Company of Dayton built many of the circus owners' private and advance railcars. The wheels for the heavy baggage and parade wagons of the golden age were fabricated by the St. Mary's Wheel Company of St. Mary, Ohio.

Originally located on Superior Street in Cleveland, the William J. Morgan & Company produced broadsheets, trade cards, pamphlets, blotters, postcards and posters to advertise local businesses. In 1887, the company was renamed Morgan Lithographic Company and focused almost entirely on the entertainment business, designing broadsheets, posters and other items for circuses, Wild West shows, theaters and traveling companies. Ringling Bros. Circus was one of its premier clients. From its work with Ringling, Morgan claimed it was the first to create billboard-size posters that required twenty-four individual lithograph sheets pasted on a wall. In the 1890s, Morgan Lithograph Company won gold medals for its large-scale posters at both the Paris World's Fair and the Chicago World's Fair. Morgan also produced political posters for William McKinley's presidential campaign in 1896.

CHAPTER 6

CIRCUS WINTER HEADQUARTERS AND OCCUPATIONAL HAZARDS

T he Sells Brothers Circus home base was located in an unincorporated area of Franklin County, Ohio, and grew to become one of the largest and finest circus winter headquarters in the country. Originally, the winter headquarters for the circus was located at the current site of the Brookside Country Club in Linworth, Ohio, just northwest of Columbus. As the show expanded, the brothers needed more land that was tillable, so they relocated to Columbus.

The headquarters, fondly referred to as "Sellsville," was picturesquely situated on the west bank of the Olentangy River, with a convenient right-of-way of the Columbus, Hocking Valley and Toledo Railroad running straight through the property. Even in the late 1880s, West Fifth Avenue in Columbus was paved, and this street marked the south boundary of the headquarters. Both the Sells and Barrett shows wintered at the site, and in time it was expanded to about one thousand acres of fertile riverfront property. The fairly self-sufficient community included living quarters, a dining hall for fifty employees, a number of large buildings to house the animals and a train shed for the railcars.

The winter headquarters of Sells Brothers Circus was regarded by local residents as being equal to the zoo in Cincinnati. At outings on Sundays, local residents and curious sightseers were allowed to visit the outstanding ring barn, where animal trainers rehearsed and exercised the show animals. The winter headquarters was an exciting place with colorful and culturally diverse residents and full of a wide variety of animals from all over the world. Much of the self-sufficiency was due to the Sells family tradition of maintaining exquisite truck gardens, orchards, a slaughterhouse and an icehouse, along with several saloons and millhouses.

The wooded area between King and West Fifth Avenues was occupied by a group of Roma (Gypsies) in the summertime, and there was a hobo village along the Hocking Valley Railroad. Hay, grain and other fodder was grown at the Sellsville site during the summer months, and this provided all of the food required for the animal stock during their winter stay. A spur off the railroad allowed parking for all of the railcars, and a large train shed provided space for making alterations and rebuilding railcars in addition to the usual maintenance and repainting of the railcars. There was also a shop that specialized in harness making and repair. The ornate parade harnesses as well as work harnesses were all fabricated by the show staff. The wagon shop was completely outfitted with two blacksmith shops and a carpentry area. Here, they made repairs on the cages, wagons, chariots and other horse-drawn vehicles.

The paint shop was nearby, and John Kueffer, a scenic artist from Cincinnati, painted historic scenes and characters on the parade wagons. Kueffer spent each winter in Columbus decorating the show. The baggage wagons were painted white and lettered in red, with the number painted on the front. The fifty men that lived in Sellsville were fed three meals a day in a dining hall, which was a converted old frame house. The men were called to dinner by the cook striking an old circular saw that served as a gong. The circus performers generally came in a few days before the season opening and stayed at downtown hotels and rooming houses.

Probably the most interesting facility within the headquarters was the ring barn, where the animals were trained and the riders practiced. This special building was divided into two sections. One section was designated to be used as a stable for the performing stock, and the other section was specifically designed as a ring identical to the one found under the circus big top. The ring was outfitted with a trainer, and training sessions were scheduled from 10:00 a.m. until 3:00 p.m. each day. William (Bud) Gorman and his wife, Polly Lee, rehearsed around 1:00 p.m. each day. The headquarters and the training sessions were open to the public on Sundays.

By 1879, the headquarters had two main departments, divided into the herbivore and the carnivore animals, along with a number of subdivisions. The main animal building was a heated facility that housed twenty-two permanent dens that provided space for the caged animals. This building was equipped with a pond of water as part of the hippopotamus cage. The elephants and other lead stock were also housed in this building. Another heated brick barn housed the lions and other big cats, camels, ape species and a wide variety of tropical birds.

Entering the building where the herbivore animals were kept, your first sight would have been a row of seven elephants, which were regarded as just very large pets. These intelligent pets liked to play tricks on those who passed by. Some examples of their trickery follow: they would steal into a person's pocket with their trunk and pull out a handkerchief, take a notebook from someone's hand or tip off their hat. Each one had a name, which he or she recognized with great familiarity. The circus had two twin elephants, smaller than the others, that were especially full of fun. The elephants required a great deal of hay and oats. It didn't take the seven elephants very long to consume a ton of hay.

The rhinoceros was also fed hay and oats and was a difficult animal to winter. Sells Brothers had an excellent specimen of rhinoceros and very close attention was given to this animal's welfare. The blue ox of India was a splendid animal. Hay and oats were also its diet. The headquarters was home to one of the finest specimens of gazelle in the country at that time, and this beautiful animal also had a diet of hay and oats. Like in the wild, the gazelle was the swiftest show animal on foot. The albino white deer was an extraordinarily beautiful animal, and the kangaroo would sit up in its stall with an anxiety that almost indicated a desire to get out and run the Australian flatlands. A very odd specimen of a species of Mexican hog was on Sunday display.

But perhaps the most remarkable animal in the collection was the African hippopotamus, and it was one of the rarest specimens in the United States at that time. This included two large adults named Dick and Babe and a baby hippopotamus. A fine ibex (wild goat), a very large zebra and an excellent sacred ox were among the collection. The only animals that were housed in open sheds were the Russian elks and the bears. For the other animals, closed housing was provided, and these buildings were kept warm by large stoves that were tended through the night. Many of the animals were from tropical climates and could not endure the cold. Their quarters were designed to be very comfortable and to prevent any losses due to cold air exposure.

There was a large collection of monkeys that relieved the monotony of winter by cutting up and playing all kinds of tricks. The monkeys were fed bread, parsnips, potatoes, turnips and almost all of the food consumed by humans except meat. They were never given meat since it was felt meat would disrupt their playful disposition. So, as a special treat, they were given fruit and candies that they very much relished.

The horse stables also housed eight large camels, several buffaloes and a large number of trained show horses. Although the camels could endure colder weather more than expected, they had to be protected during severe cold spells. They required a great deal of oats and hay. But the camels also could consume enough water at one sitting to last for some time.

Over the years, new buildings were erected and improvements were made to accommodate the annual additions to the circus. The staff devoted the winter to getting the animals in good condition and to assembling new features of entertainment for various performances. The work of preparing for a season's performances couldn't be appreciated by someone not familiar with the labor and care required to carefully train animals.

Passing along into the department of the carnivorous animals, the visitors came in contact with a number of savage beasts who were fed fresh meat daily. The show's hyena was truly a fine wild specimen. The silver lion had a ferocious roar, but he was a beautiful animal and viewed as being much finer than the common lion. There were eight ordinary lions, and a few were unusually large creatures. There was at one time a lioness with three cubs. These young animals were very docile, like kittens for a time. The attendants were with the animals constantly, and their risks with them in the cages frequently shocked the unaccustomed observer.

The carnivore building had an anteater that was a very interesting-looking creature. The staff called this anteater "the housekeeper" because upon leaving the room it was tied at the door, and there was no danger of a stranger entering while a peculiar-looking anteater was on guard. An African leopard enjoyed being caged close to the warm stove. There was also a cage for a blue-faced mandrel, which was a species of ape with a long-shaped face that could be very ferocious if agitated, but it was regarded as being more intelligent than an ordinary monkey. It would do almost anything that it was instructed to do.

The birdcages were filled with the grandest of the winged creatures. The collection had fine Australian cockatoos, Mexican parrots, golden pheasants and a number of other striking species. Sells agents would acquire most of their animals from dealers all over the country and in Europe. Quite a number of animals that belonged to the show were sent to Cincinnati to be exhibited in the Zoological Garden during the winter months. Among these were a very fine tiger and a very valuable collection of snakes. The zoo staff members often described the snakes as "treacherous things." They could become familiar with them as with the other animals, but there was no telling when they might show their treachery.

According to Jessica Sells of the Ohio History Connection and a direct descendent of the Sells brothers, one interesting point about Sellsville as a circus residential community is that periodically animals such as polar bears and elephants would escape their confinement and go on a walk-about. One home owner had his front porch demolished by a curious elephant.

A circus season would generally start in late April or early May and end sometime between late October and late November. The animals would generally have four to five months of rest off the road. A great amount of time, labor, patience and expense was required to winter such a large circus show. The wagons of the Sells Brothers were out every day hauling in produce and feed supplies. Although Sellsville was fairly self-sufficient, the establishment managers would also contract with other local farmers and vendors for supplies such as fruit and coal. During some seasons the Sells Brothers would have as many as two hundred employees on their payroll. Two locomotives were necessary to convey the show from one town to another. There were approximately thirty railcars to transport. If the show had continued to travel with just wagons by road it would have required two hundred horses. In the spring, the show would start out with many valuable additions, and it was one of the largest and best in the country.

The Sellsville winter headquarters was not just a racially integrated village but also a culturally integrated community. A perfect example of this was the children's school, located on Virginia Avenue not too far from Chambers Road. It was fondly referred to as the "Polkadot School" because the enrollment was of near equal numbers of black and white children. Many of the white children were of different European cultural backgrounds. It should be remembered that all of the Sells brothers fought for the Union during the Civil War, and many reforms in race relations were initiated by Civil War veterans. Also, during the nineteenth century, circus showmen were some of the most open-minded individuals regarding race. But due to public sentiment, they often had to segregate activities while on the road. It should also be noted that some of the older black residents of Sellsville had previously been slaves who came by way of the Underground Railroad, which was very active in Ohio prior to the Civil War.

The Antioch Baptist Church of Sellsville, Ohio, was founded by the Reverend Isaac Howell, who was originally from Virginia. The church is currently located at 1015 Chambers Road and has a predominately black congregation. Reverend Howell was also one of the founders of the Union

Grove Baptist Church on North Champion Avenue in Columbus. His life was greatly devoted to planting churches and spreading the gospel of salvation. The village had a competitive black baseball team called the Sellsville Sluggers and a twenty-one-piece band known as the Clippers, which would give Saturday afternoon concerts.

After the Ringlings acquired full title to the Forepaugh-Sells show, August and Henry Ringling were placed in charge of the Forepaugh-Sells show, and they operated out of the Sellsville Columbus location during the winter of 1906–1907 getting the show ready. But, August Ringling died during the 1907 season and most of the show's equipment was sent to Bridgeport, Connecticut, for use with the Barnum & Bailey Circus after closing on November 16, 1907, in Pine Bluff, Arkansas, and the balance of the show was then transferred to Baraboo, Wisconsin.

This was the final curtain call and the official end of the Sells Brothers Circus winter headquarters and operations in Columbus. However, the unincorporated community known as Sellsville did continue as a township community until it was finally annexed by the City of Columbus.

Unfortunately, there is no one around these days who experienced or recalls the original winter headquarters of the Old John Robinson Circus in Terrace Park, Ohio, a suburb of Cincinnati. And even worse, there are very few records and no accurate detailed descriptions of what life was like at the Robinson winter headquarters.

But what is left of the former home of the John Robinson Circus is a beautiful old three-story Italianate brick home with twenty-two rooms. Typical architectural details of the era include high ceilings and doorways and beautiful stained-glass windows. One stained-glass window on the upstairs landing once held a picture of the farm. In an upstairs bedroom are the initials *J.F.R.* inlaid in the hardwood floor, as it was "the Governor" who first lived there, and his picture is also set in the corner of the fireplace stones. In another bedroom is one of those grand old fireplaces, the woodwork of which was hand carved. The front porch grillwork is extremely ornate and resembles the ironwork found in old New Orleans. Few people today realize that most of New Orleans' old ornate iron grillwork was fabricated in Cincinnati and shipped to New Orleans on riverboats via the Ohio and Mississippi Rivers.

There was once a designated horse training barn and an elephant shed, cattle barn and monkey house. Aside from the main house, everything else was just viewed as former livestock buildings and utility sheds of no value. The original surrounding acreage was sold decades ago for suburban expansion.

In 1896, the humble town of Geneva, Ohio, had a population of three thousand. There were five churches, a funeral home, two drugstores, one dry goods store, two groceries and two clothing establishments. The town had industry that included a bicycle factory, a piano factory, a metal wheel works, a flour mill, the electric light company and a telephone system. Other commerce included two banks, two hardware stores, three jewelers, a laundry, two bakeries and two meat markets. What put Geneva on the map was that it had two railroads running through the town and was the home of the Walter L. Main Circus winter headquarters.

The demise of Walter L. Main winter headquarters in Geneva is an interesting short epic. It has a hint of eerie and prophetic results that began in 1906 when a company was formed with Fred Cummins and Sig Sautelle to be known as "Cummins' Wild West Exhibition Co.," with Walter L. Main as one of the principals. Main's name was not to be used for advertising purposes because he wanted it reserved for circus work only. At the beginning, it was agreed that it would take from $75,000 to $100,000 to put this outfit on the road. While it was understood that Cummins had no capital, Sautelle (whose real name was George C. Satterlee) declared that he would furnish the required funding for 50 percent of the stock. With this understanding, the three men proceeded. Cummins contributed about $2,600 worth of Wild West material. Sautelle shipped in some railcars, cages and wagons that went immediately into the shops for repairs and were put in good condition, but the only capital he had amounted to $800. The Sautelle material was all rushed through and loaded on the railcars ready to move out.

In the meantime, things began to look suspicious, and the Erie Lithograph Company made an attachment against Sautelle's property, on an old account, and for safety took up the switch so the railcars couldn't be moved. Finally, Main had to pay Sautelle $18,000 ($500,000 in 2018 dollars) for all of his property in Geneva to get rid of him and end the trouble.

Up to this time, Cummins, who was noted for his irregularities, behaved nobly, but he then got extremely intoxicated and never recovered from his drinking spree. This left Main alone to get the show out as best he could. In the original deal, Main was not to travel, but with Sautelle and Cummins out of the picture, Main had to assume all obligations. Much against the advice of friends and his attorneys, he placed W.W. Powers in as manager of the outfit, which consisted of twenty-seven railcars, a Wild West show and a menagerie show without a circus. This resulted in a loss of over $1,000 per day ($28,000 in 2018 dollars) until the season was two-thirds over, when Main took charge. He added circus features in the Wild West arena and added his own name to the title. The show then made money every day thereafter until the close of the season, with all people paid at the last stand at Andover, Ohio, on October 1. But many bills had accumulated during the season, amounting to over $63,000 ($1.75 million in 2018 dollars).

After the outfit arrived at Geneva and the horses were sent to the farms, D.C. Hawn, superintendent in charge, was instructed by Main not to unload or put anything in the buildings until the next day. By then, proper arrangements would be made for insurance and everything put in its right place. But contrary to those orders, the material was unloaded and placed in the winter quarters in the afternoon. That night, a fire broke out that swept everything before it, including the buildings. The total loss was over $50,000 ($1.5 million in 2018 dollars), and nothing remained except ashes. The only things that escaped were the elephants, because they were easily led from the fire.

Cummins then demanded that Main should purchase all of the company stock. He threatened to throw the stock into the hands of a receiver, which he did. Now, all of the costs of the proceedings were thrown upon Main as he was the only party who had any means and was within the jurisdiction of the court. The trial proved to be a farce because Cummins's Chicago attorney was found to be an ex-convict and disbarred from the profession. For this reason, he was not allowed to obtain any of the attorneys' fees, which were allowed by the court. Therefore, Cummins beat himself with nothing left but a tarnished name and a bankrupt pocket.

Main was out over $125,000 ($3.5 million in 2018 dollars) before all debts and costs were finally settled, but this amount is questionable because Main, as well as other old-time circus owners, was inclined to exaggerate the money he made or lost. He then determined to sell out and retire from the circus business permanently. However, he did continue to lease his name and show property to responsible parties who would keep up his established reputation. And he continued to rent the property and equipment without the use of his name.

OCCUPATIONAL HAZARDS

Working and performing with any circus could be and was often a very hazardous affair. Even general life on the road could result in death due to waterborne diseases such as typhoid. Most accidents that resulted in internal injuries would eventually cause death. But we should also bear in mind that in the post–Civil War era until 1880, the average life span was only thirty-nine years. The following details about accidents and near misses occurred with the Sells Brothers circus but were typical of most big circuses.

On May 14, 1879, in Mercer, Pennsylvania, while switching cars in the rail yard, the palace sleeper car jumped the track and startled all aboard, but there were no injuries or damage to the railcar.

During their initial visit to Kansas City, Missouri, in 1880, one of the horse teams took fright and upset the cage the horses were drawing and caused the driver to break his leg. After setting up in Des Moines, Iowa, on July 3, a grand procession and celebration was given, which included three performances to full-capacity audiences. But unfortunately, four days later, while the Sells train was sitting on a sidetrack waiting for another train to pass, people were eager to see all they could and were running over the tracks. When the train the circus was waiting for pulled up, a boy about twelve years old attempted to jump on a railcar and fell underneath the cars. The boy's hip and lower limbs were crushed, and he died that evening. Unfortunately, such tragic accidents involving the public would happen two to three times a year.

The 1881 season opened as usual in Columbus on the evening of April 26, with the audience being entertained by James Robinson, the world champion bareback rider. While he was performing, he fell from his horse and struck the back of his head and shoulders. Although he sustained severe injuries, he mounted his horse again and completed his performance with great fanfare and applause from the audience. While performing in Terre Haute, Indiana, on April 30, trapeze artist Charles Orville fell to the ground a distance of nearly twenty-five feet, striking his head and dislocating the fingers on his left hand. Although he was severely hurt, he continued with the company and was able to return to performing on the balancing trapeze. In Bellaire, Ohio, on July 2, a fatal accident occurred involving one of the wagon drivers. He ventured too near a cage containing a Bengal tiger. The unlucky man was seized and pulled against the bars of the cage, and the tiger proceeded to rip his arm off. His death was subsequently reported to the local authorities.

Toward the end of the 1881 season, in Fostoria, Ohio, on October 8, Clarice Hunting was giving a performance on the double trapeze with her husband, Robert Hunting. Mrs. Hunting attempted a routine known as the "Drop," which she had previously executed many times. During this particular attempt, she miscalculated the distance and missed her aim. She fell a distance of twenty-three feet. On the ground, in attendance to the Huntings, was Thomas Jasper. He detected the mistake and rushed forward and was able to catch Mrs. Hunting, breaking her fall. His action saved Mrs. Hunting from serious injury. The startled audience roared with applause for Jasper's courageous intervention.

And in Ottumwa, Iowa, on July 7, 1881, during a procession along the outer circle of the tent arena, one of the elephants became enraged at his keeper. The elephant lifted the man off his feet and proceeded to throw him violently to one side, but very luckily, the man was able to escape with only a few bruises.

The 1882 Sells season opened in Columbus to a crowd of over 8,000 people. On the evening of April 20, Willie Sells was concluding his performance when he slipped and fell beneath the horse's hoofs. He was trampled upon and although severely bruised, he was able to finish his act still smiling and was given resounding applause by the audience.

In Harper, Kansas, on May 14 during the Sells season of 1886, the show suffered a blowdown by the wind just as the afternoon show was about to start and the rain began to fall. The rain was accompanied by even stronger winds, and a huge gust split the top of the tent. Another followed in quick succession. This dislocated the top to such an extent that it came down and scattered the audience in all directions. Thanks to the presence of mind of a few cool heads, a full-scale stampede was averted and no one was injured. The attendees exited quickly but quietly. This, of course, ruined the afternoon performance. However, all hands went to work at once in an effort to repair the damage in time for the evening performance. By evening, the show stands were ready, and a night show was given without an overhead big top.

Also during the 1886 season, the Sells Circus pulled into Virginia City, Nevada, late on August 5, but business still proved to be very good. Edward Huff entered the tiger den during the parade and briefly lost control of the animals, and they attacked him. But with a display of skill and coolness, he was still able to humble them into submission.

In San Francisco on April 27, 1889, the evening show opened to a full capacity house. A Sells Circus performer, Josephine Ashton, equestrienne, fell from her horse while executing her principal act and was badly bruised and shaken, but upon standing was applauded by the audience.

On December 20, 1899, Patsy Forepaugh (whose real name was M.J. Meagher) who trained elephants for the circus, was at his job at the winter quarters of Forepaugh-Sells Brothers Circus in Columbus, Ohio. Patsy had been the keeper of Sid, a giant bull elephant, for many years and had no trouble with the large animal. But on this particular occasion, as the elephants were being led into the training area for their daily exercise, Sid became irritated. Forepaugh then jabbed Sid with a bull hook stick, and this only served to further fully enrage the animal. Sid grabbed Patsy with his trunk, raised him up and threw him against a wall and proceeded to kill Patsy by falling upon him and pierced him with one of his tusks. Sometime later, Sid killed another man at the Pan-American Exposition in Buffalo, New York, and another keeper while showing at Madison Square Garden. But Sid's offenses were not deemed punishable by death because it cost far less to replace a trainer versus purchasing a new elephant, and he continued to perform. Sid was finally deemed unmanageable and was executed on December 20, 1904.

In April 1896, Charles Taylor, who was a twenty-one-year-old peanut vendor turned lion tamer overnight, was attacked and severely bitten by Nero the lion, owned by the Forepaugh-Sells Brothers Circus. Nero was a very expensive acquisition for the Sells brothers because of his striking beauty and crowd-pleasing loud roar. Given the nature of this particular beast, it proved very difficult to find a tamer willing to even enter the cage with Nero, much less teach him to perform tricks. So the young and ambitious Taylor volunteered to give Nero a try. One segment of Nero's training consisted of a series of jumps over Taylor's uplifted leg. The lion successfully cleared his leg several times in succession. But during the next attempt, the lion ran toward Taylor's leg and in lieu of jumping over it, he proceeded to sink his teeth into Taylor's leg. This, of course, caused serious injury to Taylor, who survived to join a fraternity of other lion trainers who had been "bested" by Nero.

CHAPTER 7

TRAVELING HAZARDS AND TRAIN WRECKS

Railroad travel in the nineteenth century could be dangerous. In fact, the death toll resulting from rail accidents was in many ways equal in proportion to the auto accidents in the mid-twentieth century. Given the mileage logged in a season and the varied condition of the tracks and their maintenance standards, most of the big circuses experienced some kind of tragic rail disaster.

THE SELLS BROTHERS TRAIN WRECKS

On May 1, 1878, in Birmingham, Pennsylvania, three cages were knocked off a railcar and a hippopotamus got loose. The beast was quickly seized and returned to captivity with no injuries. That same year, on September 15, near Caldwell, Ohio, an elephant's railcar was derailed and one man was seriously injured.

During the 1882 season, on the night of September 21, at 2:15 a.m., the Sells Brothers Circus was en route to London, Kentucky, and taking on water at Silver Creek, a town eight miles from Richmond, Kentucky. While stopped, the circus management received a report that the first section of the circus train had been wrecked at Paint Lick, a small town just five miles farther ahead. A general order was issued for all hands to get out of bed and be ready on their feet. Everyone complied, but there were a few who doubted the report was genuine. A group of about forty proceeded toward the site of the wreck and upon arrival encountered a sight of sheer disaster. Across the tracks with his head cut in two laid the remains of the property manager J. Carter. A number of others were lying under the derailed cars and broken tableaux wagons in a bruised and mangled condition. The work of extracting the badly hurt immediately commenced, and the injured individuals were taken to the Veranda Boarding House, a short distance down the road, where they received medical attention.

During an inquiry as to the cause of the accident, the following particulars were given. The first section, which consisted of sixteen railcars, was traveling down a steep grade from Moran Summit. Since the full assembly of cars only had four brakes, the train became unmanageable and proceeded down the tracks at a terrific rate of speed. This caused the link-and-pin coupling (which is used to attach two or more railcars) to detach and fall beneath the wheels. This action then caused the third car from the engine to be thrown over an embankment and the other cars followed. In all, seven cars were completely demolished and four badly damaged. The locomotive engineer, Mr. J. Foley, stated that he was running with the engine in full reverse and applying abrasive sand to the rails and that the speed was thirty miles per hour. The railcars were the property of a private railroad company because the Sells Brother's railcars were in Elizabethtown, Kentucky, being outfitted with new flat beds. The losses were considerable as a result of the accident. The circus was not able to give the scheduled performance at London, where a large attendance was expected since this was the first time any show had ever advertised to appear in that community. But even worse was that the accident had three total fatalities that included Mr. J. Carter, Mr. R. Case and Mr. Willis Underwood. There were also fifteen people badly injured.

The most exciting, as well as amusing, incident of the wreck was the escape of the Bengal tiger, which prowled about for three hours unsupervised. Robert McCormick, who was employed with the show, was quietly resting nearby when he was aroused by something tugging at the canvas over him. He looked up and saw the two glaring eyes of the tiger looking at him. Not being daunted after such a hard morning, he just raised his hand, saying, "Go away Ben, go away." The tiger, not knowing what to make of this, just turned and walked away. But he was vigilantly watched by a number of local townsmen with loaded shotguns until he was once again securely caged.

Upon returning to the winter headquarters in Columbus, Doctor W.W. Freeman, the physician of the Sells Brothers Circus, was presented with a diamond-set gold medal in appreciation for his service to the company employees and his many friends during the accident.

In 1886, on August 6, following the Virginia City showing, the Sells Circus train was packed up and began making its way to Carson City. While en route, the train got away from the engineer and made its way down a hill at sixty miles per hour. Sleeper car no. 3 struck a trestle, which woke up everyone with an initial startle that quickly elevated into tremendous fright. Everyone considered jumping off the train until car no. 3 finally ran off the track at the river, where it was quickly abandoned and left behind.

1884 S.H. BARRETT TRAIN WRECKS

The most extended period of misfortune in circus rail transport followed the S.H. Barrett Circus in 1884. This show was a second, smaller circus owned by the Sells Brothers Circus of Columbus, Ohio, and suffered losses in five wrecks, four of which occurred in a twenty-five-day period during April and May, beginning with Harrodsburg, Kentucky, on April 10. The next was Abington, Virginia, on April 19. The Williamsburg, Kentucky railcar incident followed on April 30, and four days later, an accident occurred in Bardstown, Kentucky, on May 3. Two months later into the season, another rail accident occurred in Stuart, Iowa, on July 2. The great fortune was that no injuries were incurred during this rash of railroad mishaps.

JOHN ROBINSON CIRCUS TRAIN WRECKS

At Fergus Falls, Minnesota, on October 4, 1885, at 2:00 a.m., an accident occurred on the Northern Pacific Railroad, Black Hills Division. The John Robinson Circus and menagerie left Wahpeton, North Dakota, in two sections. As the first train approached the summit of the steep hill about six miles west of Fergus Falls, Minnesota, the caboose and two sleeper cars containing about 150 circus employees became detached. The railcars proceeded back down the hill at a fearful speed, with insufficient braking power. The engineer of the second section, which was only about a mile behind, saw the impending danger but set the brakes so tightly they could not be readily released. Otherwise, the engineer may have been able to reverse his train and avoid a collision. The three cars were smashed beyond recognition, and beneath the debris, over 100 human beings were completely buried. People in the second section immediately came to the rescue. Word was sent to Fergus Falls for help, which was immediately dispatched by the rail superintendent and his assistants, with heavy equipment to lift wrecked train debris. Since it was extremely dark and very cold, the rescue work was extremely laborious.

There were five killed outright, and three others died days later. Eleven people were otherwise injured but lived to tell of their experience. James Wilson, a train watchman and former policeman from Cincinnati, Ohio, was killed trying to warn the sleeping crew of the danger of the collision. Although he was aware that the collision was inevitable, he refused to desert. He was frightfully mangled, as his heart was found on top of a flatcar some distance away, his bowels lying on the ground and his body cut to pieces. One man was rescued uninjured, wedged in the debris between two dead bodies. All who were killed were teamsters or workers in the employ of the John Robinson show. The railroad officials greatly regretted the unavoidable loss of life. The injured men received every care and attention. Since there was no damage to the show property, the engagements scheduled for Fergus Falls the following day and at Brainerd that coming Tuesday were given as advertised.

In St. Louis, Missouri, on November 4, 1887, the John Robinson Circus train had just arrived at the St. Louis Union Station from Fort Scott, Kansas, where the last stand had been made. Its destination was the winter headquarters in Cincinnati, Ohio. The train consisted of twenty flatcars, carrying animal cages and circus paraphernalia, and three passenger coaches for performers and employees. It stopped in the Missouri Pacific yards, and when the signal to start was given, the train pulled out rapidly toward the bridge. As one of the front cars was passing over the "puzzle switch," it jumped the track, and the cars and cages in the rear dashed over it and collided with a freight train going in the opposite direction. The wreck killed a canvas man named James Squires, and two others, named Fuller and Isle, were critically injured.

A pair of lions, a tiger, a leopard and a hyena succeeded in escaping from the cages. The excitement was intense for a few minutes, but the animals, being of the circus kind, were just as scared as the people and were easily captured. The lion cage was shattered, and the lion and his consort leaped out onto the track and circled the wreck twice, and when the people fled, terror-stricken, the lions did likewise. They crawled under the wreck, leaving only their tails visible. The tiger made a beeline for the baggage room and took refuge behind some trunks. The hyena dodged under a freight car and howled. The leopard ran around for a few minutes and knocked a couple of men over and then jumped back into the wrecked cage.

The lion tamer was the first man to the rescue. He grabbed the African monarch lion by the tail and dragged him out from under the wreck and tossed him into another cage. Then he seized the female lioness by the tail and neck and led her into the cage. They both appeared grateful to him for the protection he gave them. They had never seen the jungle and were not viciously bad animals. One scared bystander started shooting at the tiger until the lion tamer took the frightened beast by the neck and led him into a boxcar. The hyena meanwhile had been stoned by some boys and was howling mournfully when rescued. A big boa constrictor was cut to pieces under the wheels of a car, and two mountain lions were also killed. The tiger was shot in three places, and the hyena lost half his tail. A pair of ibex goats were also killed, and half a dozen monkeys were never found.

The John Robinson Circus while still making its way back to Cincinnati was involved in another serious train wreck the following day on November 5 at Brazil, Indiana. The following year, in 1888, the John Robinson show had a train wreck near Corwin, Ohio, on September 10.

WALTER L. MAIN CIRCUS TRAIN WRECK

On Tuesday morning, May 30, 1893, about 5:30 a.m., the engineer of Walter L. Main's circus train lost control of the locomotive while proceeding down the mountain on the Tyrone & Clearfield Railway. Earlier that day, engine No. 1500 was selected to draw the circus train, with Stephen Croswell as the engineer and Harvey Meese serving as fireman. When Osceola, Pennsylvania, was reached, in order to make the ascent of the mountain, another engine was attached at the rear as a pusher. The ascent was achieved safely. When the summit was reached, and the pusher left the train on its trip down the hillside, the circus train containing its passengers and cargo of animals and equipment just took off down the mountain. The train rounded a dozen or more short curves at a high rate of speed. One witness later stated the train was going so fast that one couldn't count the telegraph poles as the train seemed to be literally flying down the mountain. A mile or two down the mountain, there was a reverse curve and then a mile of straight track to Vail

Station. It was at the Tyrone end of the reverse curve, where the train was in a wild ride and picking up more speed, that nineteen of the railcars filled with people and animals jumped from the tracks and were broken to pieces.

The destination of that Main circus was Lewistown, Pennsylvania. It was composed of twenty-two circus railcars. The route lay over the Tyrone & Clearfield branch of the Pennsylvania Railroad. Luckily, the locomotive and passenger coaches remained on the rails. Often, many of the men slept in the cars under the wagons containing the animals. Sixteen animal cages, along with the railcars, were completely demolished, and pandemonium reigned. The dead and wounded people were taken from the wreck, and the wounded were removed to the hospital.

Frank Train was the treasurer of the company and had resigned Saturday, May 27, but when Walter Main asked him to continue until the show reached Lewistown on May 30, he agreed. Frank always occupied and slept in his usual place, which was in his ticket wagon that was loaded on a railcar near the center of the train. This was a common practice to prevent the ticket wagon from being robbed. He was the first person looked after because he was still alive but pinned down under a mass of heavy wreckage, and everyone labored faithfully to release him. It was two hours before he could be reached. At times, he would urge his rescuers to hurry if they wanted to get him out alive. He died just as he was being taken out of the wreckage.

When the wild animals got loose, a strange spectacle was witnessed. The head of one of the elephants was pinned down by one of the cars. Upon being freed, the huge elephant struggled to his feet, shaking off the heavy timbers like straw, and plowed through the balance of the wreck to freedom, seemingly happy at his escape.

One of the tigers got out, and in this case immediately began looking around to see what he could devour. He pounced upon the sacred ox, which had been badly wounded and tore it frightfully, killing it. The tiger then headed out into the countryside, looking for new fields. He came to the farm of Alfred Thomas, where Thomas's wife was milking a cow. She left suddenly and the tiger sprang upon the cow she was milking and killed it. He was devouring his quivering meal when the farmer Thomas appeared with his rifle and shot the tiger. Pleased with his royal sport, farmer Thomas shouldered his rifle and started in pursuit of a panther that he knew was cavorting on the mountainside. He failed to find the wild jungle cat, which remained at large.

One lion continued freely roaming the woods, but the other lion was captured easily by its trainer. He tied a rope around its neck and secured it

This photo of the 1893 Tyrone train wreck shows the derailed flats that carried the wagon and tableaux. *Tyrone-Snyder Public Library.*

to a log, where it stayed quietly the rest of the day looking at the turbulent scene below. Keeper Jenks was endeavoring to subdue a lion when the ferocious cat seized him and tore off his kneecap. The water buffalo, two camels, a dromedary, two elephants, a zebra, yak, hyena and many small animals from different parts of the world did not wander far from the wreck, although they were unrestrained. All the animals that were saved roamed around loose, seemed content with their freedom and didn't care to abuse it by running off. Many of the smaller animals were not injured, though their cages were crushed about them. None of them seemed at all nervous or excited but browsed contentedly or wallowed in the creek nearby as though it was an everyday occurrence.

A sizable number of chattering monkeys escaped to the trees, where they looked down in wonder at the wreckage. But they were soon calmed by sweetmeats and captured. The dying groans of some of the trained horses were sorrowful, and most of them were pulled out only to be shot because their limbs were broken or they were fatally injured. Five pure white horses, all elegant performers, representing years of patience and teaching, had to be slain. In all, sixty-eight horses were known to have been killed, including nearly the entire collection of valuable ring and trick horses. This included the trick horses Chicago and Flake, the white leader of Joe Berris's six-horse team, together with all the valuable horses ridden by Tony Lowande. Flake was badly wounded and lay carefully bedded and covered by an awning, breathing heavily. Every so often, he made an attempt to rise, and when the attendant would place his hand on the horse's head, it would lie back down. The alligators were stretched on the ground as if dead, but a rub along the nose with a stick would show them wide awake.

To illustrate the thoroughness of the wreckage, all of the show wagons were completely destroyed, in addition to nineteen railcars. The only one retaining even the shape of a railcar was the one containing the elephants, and it had to be cut to pieces in order to release the huge pachyderms. The car laid on its side, and through the two openings the elephants and their attendants were taken out, all more or less bruised, cut and bleeding, but not seriously injured. One of the elephants had broken one of its front legs.

THE RAILS SPREAD

Regarding the follow-up investigation, there seems to be no doubt that the train ran away and it was beyond the power of the engineer to control. Whether the brakes would not hold or whether the fault was not furnishing another engine was never determined.

One report has it that an axle on the tender broke, but after a careful comprehensive examination of the wreck and wreck site, it was determined that the rails spreading caused the derailment. Given the speed and momentum of the fast-running train, when the engine left the curve and entered the straight track, this produced a force that caused the rails to spread. This resulted in the locomotive tender car dropping onto the rail ties and causing the disastrous derailment. The engine remained on the track, but quickly following the tender over the twenty-foot embankment on the left-hand side of the road came every railcar in the train, except the four passenger coaches in the rear.

Although the accident was devastating, by some good fortune, the passenger coaches were brought to a sudden stop as soon as the engine separated from the tender. From the first coach, Main could immediately see the destruction that had taken place. He rallied his entire crew and proceeded at once to rescue those who were pinned beneath the wreckage. The fifteen cars were a mass of kindling, and in length the debris occupied

This photo shows the curve where the Walter L. Main Circus train derail occurred. The momentum of the high rate of speed caused the track to spread and the wheels to jump the tracks. 1893. *Tyrone-Snyder Public Library.*

a distance equal to about five railcars. Main was too busily engaged looking after the comfort of his employees and trying to save whatever of his property he could to talk about the wreck. All the wrecked cars were a total loss.

Another fatality had occurred at the scene of the disaster that involved a local resident. While working with a wrecking crew, in the effort to remove debris, a rope, which was attached to a tank for the purpose of pulling it up the bank, broke and struck Robert M. Gates on the chest. His injuries proved serious, and he died within an hour of the accident. The unfortunate victim, age twenty-eight, was engaged to be married and was a resident of Tyrone.

As stated earlier, railroad accidents resulting in deaths were a common occurrence in the later nineteenth century. One big reason had to do with the ability to control the speed of an extended train, particularly on downhill grades. George Westinghouse (1846–1914) developed an air braking system that greatly increased rail travel safety by allowing the engine and all attached railcars to stop at the same time.

The locomotive brakes were part of the problem that caused the Walter L. Main Circus Tyrone disaster. Granville T. Woods (1856–1910) was an African American inventor who held more than sixty patents. Born in

Columbus, Ohio, Woods dedicated his life to developing a variety of inventions relating to the railroad industry. In 1884, he received his first patent, for a more efficient version of a steam boiler furnace. That same year, along with the help of his brother Lyates Woods, he established the Woods Electric Company in Cincinnati, Ohio, to produce and market his own inventions. Most of his work was on trains and streetcars. Woods invented the Multiplex Telegraph, a device that sends messages between train stations and moving trains and helped prevent deadly train collisions. In addition to the Multiplex Telegraph, he also was issued a patent for improvements to the conventional rail air brake system. The Westinghouse Air Brake Company later purchased this patent from Woods.

CHAPTER 8

THE COMPETITIVE PRODIGAL NEPHEW WILLIE SELLS

William "Willie" Sells (1865?–1908) was an expert bareback horse rider and showman who was the adopted son of Allen Sells. Willie began as an equestrian for that circus and became a prominent four-horse rider (standing on two horses' backs and controlling four horses at once). He achieved early fame as a ten-year-old bareback rider with the 1876 season of the Sells Brothers Great European Zoological Institute and Equestrian Exposition. As a young man, he was renowned as "The Chesterfield of the Arena" and had developed a proclivity for fast living beyond his means. As a result, his contract was not renewed by the Sells Brothers Circus at the end of the 1889 season, and this supposedly initiated an estrangement between Allen and his brothers that remained until Allen's death in 1894. Previously in 1883, the Sells brothers bought out the interest of Willie's father, Allen Sells, for $40,000 ($1 million in 2018 dollars) with the understanding that he would not enter into show business again as a competitor.

The following season, Willie signed with Barnum & Bailey for its 1889–90 London engagement but proved to be a disappointment due to repeatedly missing show performances. Also due to his overindulgences, he lost control of his weight and became too heavy to ride. He therefore decided to abandon the ring and pursued a career as a circus manager.

Taking full advantage of his family name, Willie decided to start several shows of his own, one being Sells Olympian Shows with Andrew Morris. He started Sells and Rentfrow Show, with Jasper N. Rentfrow as his partner. While the Sells Show was in Australia, Willie and Rentfrow took full advantage

Willie Sells made a point of using the Sells name after he had agreed not to. He used the name to his advantage as a self-promoting circus owner in a variety of different partnerships that eventually failed. Circa 1880. *Cincinnati Art Museum.*

and worked the original regular Sells Brothers Circus midwestern territory.

Ephraim, Lewis and Peter, who were the actual owners of the famous Sells Brothers Circus, were furious and embarrassed by their nephew's actions, which identified the Sells name with the worst kinds of illicit game of chance and shortchanging customers. Willie's effort to create the impression that his show was the original Sells Brothers Enormous Show was undermining the reputation and credibility that the brothers had worked to establish for nearly thirty years. After returning from their Australian tour, the Sells brothers countered Willie's audacity by launching a full-scale public relations campaign in practically every community that Willie had played a stand. In 1893, Sells and Rentfrow filed a civil suit against the Sells brothers, asking for $48,000 ($1.33 million in 2018 dollars) in damages due to losses as a result of the Sellses' advertising against their show. In the end, the case was settled out of court for $4,000 ($110,000 in 2018 dollars). Local newspapers at the time reported that as part of the settlement, Willie had to agree to discontinue using the Sells name, but this is highly questionable.

Willie's father, Allen Sells, died an extremely wealthy man on March 20, 1894. Willie, of course, thought that he would become lord of the manor by inheriting everything and taking care of his mother in the meantime. Allen's funeral was three days later, but Lewis and Peter did not attend the funeral or acknowledge the death of their brother. This was mainly due to the estrangement caused by Willie. Ephraim and three of the Sells sisters, however, did attend the service.

Allen's will was opened and read in Shawnee County probate court on March 31. To Willie's astonishment, everything that his father possessed was, without exception, left to his wife, Sarah Ann Sells. She was also designated to be the executrix of the full estate—and proved to be a capable administrator. The Columbus Sells brothers were also very capable businessmen. But all of their prudence and good business sense could not protect the Sells family and reputation from Willie Sells.

Following the death of Ephraim Sells, who died in Columbus on August 1, 1898, of Bright's disease, Willie Sells filed another suit against Lewis and Peter Sells for $150,000 ($1.5 million in 2018 dollars) in damages in the district court at Topeka, Kansas. As the plaintiff, he claimed that at various times when he attempted to form a partnership with various investors, the Sells brothers would harass and threaten legal action that resulted in Willie losing potential financial backers. The Sells brothers countered by stating Willie's name was not really Sells. Willie refuted the argument by stating the Sells Brothers Circus advertised him for a number of years as Willie Sells, champion bareback rider of the world. In nineteenth-century America, children were often taken in and cared for in another family without legal proceedings and were recognized by their community as being adopted, but there is no birth record of Willie's actual name. He was probably a Civil War orphan.

He had, at one time or another, interest in Hummel, Hamilton & Sells Shows, 1897; and Great William Sells Shows United with James H. Gray New Olympian Hippodrome, 1900. The Sells & Gray Circus came to grief at the end of the 1901 season and was sold at sheriff's auction, in Algiers, Louisiana, bringing a return of $7,625. From 1899 to 1901, Willie was a fairly competent general agent while working for Walter L. Main. He also partnered with Martin Downs in the Great William Sells & Downs Consolidated Shows from 1902 to 1905.

Willie was briefly connected with the Sells-Floto Circus, which was owned by Harry H. Tammen (1856–1924) and Frederick Gilmer Bonfils (1860–1933), who was also the owner of the *Denver Post* newspaper. In 1902, Tammen and Bonfils decided to start a circus. The circus was titled the "Otto Floto Dog and Pony Show." In 1906, Tammen and Bonfils hired Willie Sells to manage the show and take full advantage of the general public's familiarity with the Sells name. To boost the reputation of his operation, Tammen quickly renamed the show the "Sells-Floto Circus." Willie was dismissed from the show by Tammen before the end of the season for reasons unknown. Willie had claimed that he had been hired in exchange for the use of his name and $100 a week plus expenses. At age forty-three, Willie Sells died of a hemorrhage of the stomach at his home in New York City on February 17, 1908.

In addition to Willie Sells's entrepreneurial misbehavior, the unsuccessful battles with the Ringling brothers and the general economic conditions in 1894 and 1895 caused the Sells Brothers Circus to look for further help to continue in business. During the winter of 1895–96, former competitor James A. Bailey acquired a one-third interest in the show, in exchange for the use of the Adam Forepaugh title and some financial assistance. As mentioned in chapter 3, the following year, 1897, James A. Bailey sold one-half of his interest in the show to William W. Cole and used the funds for shipping the Barnum & Bailey show to Europe.

Also, upon the death of Ephraim Sells in 1898, the ownership of the circus was redistributed to give Lewis and Peter Sells, W.W. Cole and James A. Bailey each an equal one-quarter share of the business.

CHAPTER 9

THE TWENTIETH-CENTURY SHOW MERGERS AND OTHER CIRCUSES

Prior to the sale of the Forepaugh & Sells Brothers Circus on January 10, 1905, Lewis Sells had received an offer from James A. Bailey that morning, after he had reached the Columbus winter headquarters. Based on the offer, Mr. Sells and Mr. Cole (Chilly Billy) both agreed to sell the show in its entirety. Following the sale, Otto Ringling left the winter quarters with Bailey and went into conference with him at the Chittenden Hotel in downtown Columbus. Bailey later announced that he had sold a one-half interest in the Forepaugh & Sells Brothers Circus to the Ringling brothers and the show would be operated jointly by Bailey and the Ringlings. Such an announcement made the small and medium show owners uncomfortable. This news meant that instead of one show leaving the road, there would be three big rail shows working in collaboration. Bailey and the Ringlings negotiated a deal whereby they divided up the country between their shows. The territory routes had Ringling Bros. opening in Chicago and working east, while Barnum and Bailey would open in New York and work westward. This left Forepaugh-Sells to open in Columbus and proceed through the Midwest and South. This acquisition made James A. Bailey the largest show owner in the circus world.

In 1906, Bailey died and the Ringlings were able to acquire Bailey's part of the Forepaugh-Sells circus holdings on July 1, 1906. This meant they bought the Bailey interest in the Forepaugh-Sells that year and the remaining shares of the Barnum & Bailey Circus in 1907. They sent the Sells outfit on tour in

1907, 1910 and 1911, the last years that the circus toured under the name Sells Brothers. The Columbus headquarters was closed by 1908 and the show was merged as part of the empire of the Ringling Bros., Barnum & Bailey circus empire but was taken off the road after 1911.

In September 1929, the American Circus Corporation (which included the Sells Floto Circus) was purchased by John Nicholas Ringling for $1.7 million ($25 million in 2018 dollars). Unfortunately for John Ringling, the Wall Street stock market crash occurred the following month. But with these acquisitions, Ringling now controlled and owned virtually all of the large traveling circuses in the country. But the Great Depression, coupled with John Nicholas Ringling's ill health, caused the Ringling empire to experience some hard times. In 1935, Ringling Bros. and Barnum & Bailey management combined the two show names of the Hagenbeck & Wallace and the Forepaugh-Sells Brothers circus for copyright protection. The latter finally ceased all operations three years later, in 1938.

John Nicholas Ringling purchased the many of the late nineteenth-century circus empires, including Barnum & Bailey, which owned Forepaugh-Sells. Ringling closed the deal for the American Circus Corporation with Jerry Mugivan a month prior to the 1929 New York stock market crash. Circa 1910. *Columbus Metropolitan Library.*

AMERICAN CIRCUS CORPORATION

Jeremiah "Jerry" Mugivan (1873–1930) of Knightsville, Indiana, began his working career selling newspapers on the train from Terre Haute to Indianapolis. He later worked as a candy vendor on the St. Louis, Iron Mountain & Southern Railway. In 1896, while employed with the railroad, Mugivan met and began talking with a passenger who turned out to be John Robinson, owner of the Ohio-based John Robinson Circus, one of the largest circuses in America at that time.

John Robinson decided to hire the young Mugivan as a ticket seller and as one of the show's advance men. After the Robinson circus, Mugivan went to work for the Sanger & Lentz traveling menagerie. At this point, he met Albert C. "Bert" Bowers, who would become a lifelong friend. The two friends went on to work for Sands & Astley Circus, Sells & Gray and the Great Wallace Shows. In 1904, Mugivan and Bowers jointly purchased the railroad circus Howes Great London Show for $3,000 ($83,000 in 2018 dollars) and renamed the circus the Great Van Amburgh Shows.

Carl Hagenbeck (1844–1913) was an internationally known German animal dealer and trainer who controlled animals by befriending them, emphasizing their intelligence for the audience. He is credited with pioneering the prototype for the modern open-air zoo with animals housed using enclosures that are closer to their natural habitats. Hagenbeck also trained animals for his own circuses at the World's Columbian Exposition in Chicago in 1893 and the Louisiana Purchase Exposition in St. Louis in 1904. Hagenbeck's circus was one of the most popular attractions. The American office of the Carl Hagenbeck Company was located at the Cincinnati Zoo, which was privately owned at the time. Sol Stephen, who served as Hagenbeck's American representative, was also director of the zoo. A newly outfitted Carl Hagenbeck Trained Animal Show was established in Cincinnati with circus wagons built by the local Bode Wagon Company. The first show went on the road for the 1905 season. This circus was equally owned by C. Lee Williams, Carl Hagenbeck, John H. Havlin and Frank R. Tate.

In 1907, Ben Wallace of Peru, Indiana, acquired controlling interest in the Carl Hagenbeck Circus. Wallace was well acquainted with Mugivan from his years on the Great Wallace Shows. Wallace gave Mugivan an interest in the new Hagenbeck-Wallace Circus in exchange for his skill and service as a show manager. Together, Mugivan and Bowers began to purchase other circuses, and in March 1916 the John Robinson Ten Big Shows was bought from "Gov." John F. Robinson of Terrace Park, Ohio.

The Great Flood of 1913 nearly destroyed the Hagenbeck-Wallace Circus winter headquarters near the Wabash River in northeastern Indiana. Major equipment and show animals, including eight elephants, twenty-one lions and tigers and eight performing horses, were lost as a result of the flood. Following the flood, the circus was sold to West Baden, Indiana businessman Ed Ballard.

Under Ballard's ownership, the circus suffered a train wreck that was worse than the Walter L. Main Tyrone incident. On June 22, 1918, toward the end of World War I, a locomotive engineer fell asleep and rammed an empty troop train into the rear of the Hagenbeck-Wallace circus train near Hammond, Indiana. The upset kerosene lamps in the sleeping railcars started fires that rapidly spread through the railcars. The collision and fire left 84 people dead and another 127 injured, and once again a sizable number of animals was lost along with equipment. After the train wreck, the show went into receivership and Mugivan and Bowers were able to acquire the Hagenbeck-Wallace Circus at auction. In 1920, Mugivan and Bowers invited Ballard to join them, and together the three established the American Circus Corporation.

In 1920, the Sells-Floto Circus was acquired by the American Circus Company from the original owners, Harry H. Tammen and Frederick G. Bonfils. The title "Buffalo Bill Wild West Show" was also included, and "Yankee Robinson" was acquired in a later purchase. The Buffalo Bill title was used along with the Sells-Floto Circus, but the Yankee Robinson title was dropped completely. The Sparks Circus, which was one of the best names in the business, was purchased in late 1928, along with Al. G. Barnes Trained Animal Show the same year.

The American Circus Corporation was now the owner of a significant and important group of circuses and several valuable titles, with the exception of those under the control of the Ringling brothers. Four months following the 1929 sale of the American Circus Corporation to John N. Ringling, Jerry Mugivan died on January 22, 1930, at the age of fifty-six. His partner Bert Bowers died six years later in January 1936.

HEBER BROTHERS GREATER SHOW CIRCUS

Not too far from the former Sells Brothers winter headquarters and on the opposite side of the Olentangy River was the Heber Brothers Greater Show Circus. Its headquarters address was 312 East Seventeenth Avenue. It was started by the Columbus-based family of Reginald "Pop" Heber in 1907 and operated primarily in the Midwest states for ten years, until about the time the United States entered World War I. Most of the performers were family members. Brothers Reginald Heber Jr. and Ben C. Heber Sr. would perform in their Scottish outfits. Avanell was a talented artist in addition to being a juggler and performer. George Heber was well known as a clown, and Rollo Heber was a trapeze performer.

The Hebers owned a printing shop and produced their own advertisements and billboard sheets. As a supervisor, Ben C. Heber Sr. was known for recruiting a group of local boys to fill in as the billboard crew. Heber Brothers

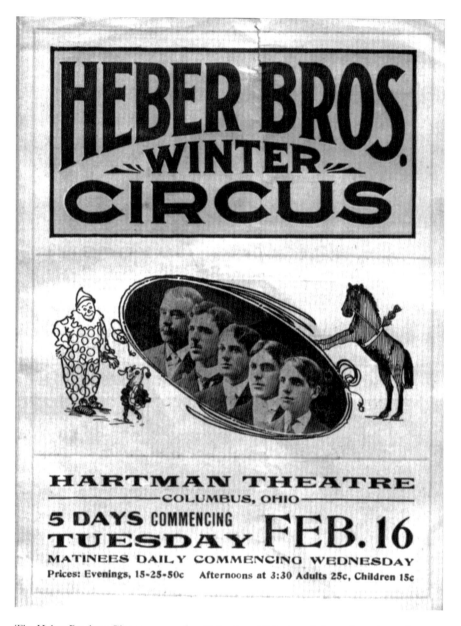

The Heber Brothers Circus was another Columbus, Ohio–based circus that wintered just east of the current University District off Seventeenth Avenue. Circa 1914. *Columbus Metropolitan Library.*

was also known for briefly having the world's largest Bactrian camel. One of the featured attractions of the Heber Brothers Greater Show Circus was Jocko the Monkey, who was raised from a baby by Adell Heber, who was married to George Heber. Adell was a lover of animals, and the Hebers' show featured an act known as the Dogs of Dogville that was a favorite for children. George was also known for featuring a dog named Nipper as part of his clown act.

THE SEILS-STERLING CIRCUS

The following was not an Ohio circus but is included to illustrate the significance and power of the nineteenth-century Ohio Sells Brothers circus name and reputation well into the first half of the twentieth century. The Sells name, along with Robinson and others, is a part of America's entertainment and cultural heritage.

The three Sheboygan, Wisconsin Lindemann brothers (William, Peter and Albert) understood the value of the Sells name. They established a show known as the Seils-Sterling Circus, which mostly played stands in the Midwest from 1924 until 1938. William Lindemann and his wife, Millie, were high-wire performers. His brother Peter and his wife, Louise, were trapeze performers. As performing artists, they spent their early careers signing to perform with various circuses, such as Yankee Robinson, Gentry Brothers and Forepaugh-Sells Brothers.

Once the brothers decided to establish their own circus, they initially used various names for the show. Their first year of business was 1911, and they titled the show the Lindemann Brothers Circus, followed by the Lindemann Big Society Circus in 1912. In 1913, Bill and Pete were joined by their brother Al, who also became a partner in the business.

In 1920, they purchased three Ford Model T trucks and created one of the first motorized traveling troupes in the country. They titled this new show the Yankee American and Lindemann Brothers Combined Show, which took place inside an eight-hundred-seat big top tent. By 1923, they decided to rename the circus the Great Danby Show, but this action didn't meet their expectations of increased ticket sales.

So for their 1924 season, they selected Seils-Sterling as the perfect title to attract the public's attention and to take advantage of the Sells Brothers Circus's reputation, which was still well remembered, respected and valuable in the circus business. But they overlooked the fact that the Ringling brothers had acquired all rights to the name when they purchased Forepaugh-Sells Brothers from James Bailey short before his death. The Ringlings threatened to take legal action. So the Lindemanns opted to just remove the bottom of the first *L* in "SELLS" to make it read "SEILS-STERLING CIRCUS." This put a quick end to any claim the Ringlings could file. It also spared the Lindemanns the cost of making any expensive alterations to the new gold-leafed lettering on their signage, trucks and wagons. The company grew throughout the 1920s and 1930s, requiring seventy vehicles to move the full show. But, as the Great Depression of the 1930s continued, the Seils-Sterling Circus was finally shut down in 1938.

FRED J. MACK CIRCUS

In the fall of 1954, Don McCullough, an acrobat and juggler with professional circus experience, approached his longtime friend and Columbus businessman Fred D. Pfening Jr. (1925–2010) about putting a tent circus on the road that following spring. In a moment of weakness, Pfening agreed, and thus began the odyssey of the Fred J. Mack Circus.

The troupe originally went by the name "The Don Mack Circus," which was McCullough's stage name. But that title had to be changed because a local television personality and outdoor writer named Don Mack filed a restraining order forbidding the use of his name. So the name was amended to read "The Fred J. Mack Circus." The "Fred" was for Pfening; the "J." was for Joe Flynn, a stockholder; and the "Mack" for McCullough.

Pfening proceeded to convince several business friends to invest in the circus. The stockholders included a Buick dealer, a veterinarian, a potato chip manufacturer, a CPA, an attorney and an insurance agent, among others. Pfening served as president and McCullough was vice president of the parent company, Public Enterprise, Inc. A little over $25,000 ($233,000 in 2018 dollars) was raised through the stock sale. As often happens with new circuses, this amount turned out to not be enough, so a few stockholders loaned the company money and a bank loan was secured. After spending $40,000 ($373,000 in 2018 dollars), the circus was ready for its premiere.

Pfening took an active role in the circus's management. While McCullough booked the acts, Pfening took care of the advertising and publicity and oversaw the acquisition of capital equipment. He also dealt with the major vendors, and most of the transport vehicles were modified or fabricated at his family's business, the Fred D. Pfening Company, which is still in operation today.

Pfening was also heavily involved in framing the physical size of the Fred J. Mack Circus. The show was transported using trucks and employed approximately seventy people. It was transported using ten show-owned vehicles and spent a little over $4,300 ($40,000 in 2018 dollars) on the trucks and trailers, which were then modified, refurnished and painted at the Pfening Company at a cost of $2,280 ($21,500 in 2018 dollars). The most unique was the office and ticket truck that previously had been a mobile X-ray unit that screened for tuberculosis. It was purchased from the State of Ohio for $250 ($2,950 in 2018 dollars). The show had two automatic stake drivers and used a farm tractor the first few days. The pole semi was specially built and allowed the poles to be loaded from the side, rather than overhead. The stake drivers were loaded in the back of the pole truck, which was a former auto transport vehicle. The canvas semi was also specially built. The tents, poles and rigging were purchased new for $6,000 ($56,000 in 2018 dollars) from the United States Tent and Awning Company in Chicago.

In mid-April 1955, the Great Fred J. Mack 3 Ring Circus had its initial opening at Don Casto's Northern Lights Shopping Center on Cleveland Avenue to a 75 percent afternoon crowd and a full night house.

The show was presented in a new blue and tangerine seventy-foot big top tent with two thirty-foot and one forty-foot tents. The marquee was in matching colors, and a grandstand was used with six hundred new folding chairs. The music was furnished by a state-of-the-art hi-fidelity record player using three turntables mounted in a sound truck.

The show was staffed with good, down-to-earth show talent. Chief Clarence Keys was the boss canvas man and his wife, Tillie, was in charge of the cookhouse. Frank Bland was the general agent, and promotion directors were used in about half of the town settings. George Hubler was the concession manager, and Orlo Sparton was the program director, who kept things moving.

There were also many well-known show people with the Fred J. Mack Circus. The great aerialist Mickey King was the most famous and the headliner. Other performers were the Orlo Sparton family, who did perch pole, neck swing, low wire and Roman rings; the George Barton family, with horses, ponies and dogs; L.B. "Doc" Ford and his wife, with ponies and dogs; Walter Harter, with dogs; Happy Spitzer, with his January mule act; and

R.A. Miller and Frankie Lou Woods, with Jesse the elephant. Mr. and Mrs. Al Ross and Georgie Lake clowned.

The midway was lit with flashing lights with a thirty-foot straight ticket-office wagon and had a full-sized clown painted on each side. The sideshow included an animal exhibit operated by R.A. Miller, of the Fort Ware Game Farm. A ride on the baby elephant Jessie was included with the $0.25 admission price ($2.50 in 2018 dollars). A twenty-by-thirty-foot display top and three concession tops filled out the midway.

Hal Eifert of the Gooding Carnival helped Pfening secure a deal with the Coca-Cola Company in which Coke got a quarter-page ad in the courier in exchange for extensive concessions equipment. Also through an advertising agreement, Coca-Cola acted as a supplier for the Mack circus by furnishing all masking curtains and end pieces for the reserve areas. This, with the blue tent, gave the show a festive, bright and colorful appearance to the big top interior.

The show used window cards and heralds, and the heralds were printed by Chief Printing, headed by the old showman R.H. Harvey of Perry, Iowa. They were loaded with old-time circus material fashioned like the printed ads used in the 1920s and '30s.

A number of block ticket sales were made in advance at various Columbus shopping center stands, and this required three shows a day. After the Columbus week, the show moved to one-day stands on a sponsored basis. Performances generally ran close to one hour and forty-five minutes.

The initial Columbus show opened on April 18 and ran until April 23, playing at four Columbus shopping centers. The show then made a 122-mile Sunday run to St. Clairsville, near the Ohio River.

From April 26 to July 5, the show played various stands in Pennsylvania, West Virginia and back in Ohio. The Fred J. Mack Circus presented a very strong show for its size but unfortunately was out for just one short season. The final performance was held in Windham, Ohio, on July 5, when the show took in $314.33 ($2,950 in 2018 dollars) playing only an evening performance.

Pfening attributed the closing of the show to the lack of an experienced advance team working out ahead of the show. In reality, the show should have had sixty to ninety days booked in advance of departing from the winter quarters, and there should have been a biller ad two weeks ahead of each show stand. The final profit and loss statement showed that in its short life the Fred J. Mack circus took in a little over $42,000 and incurred slightly less than $64,000 in expenses for a loss of close to $22,000. Like many new start-ups, the show was under-capitalized. Overall, the well-meaning effort simply lacked seasoned and experienced management.

Following his experience with the Fred J. Mack Circus, Fred D. Pfening decided it was more cost-effective and just as rewarding to study the circus as a historian instead of owning and operating one. Over the next fifty-five years, he compiled two route books each for the Cristiani and Beatty Cole Circuses and remained friends with many in the circus community. He also wrote over one hundred articles on circuses and edited *Bandwagon* magazine for the last forty-nine years of his life. Pfennig's experience with the Fred J. Mack Circus gave him an increased appreciation and respect for the difficulty of successfully operating a touring tented circus. He always expressed admiration for successful showmen and sympathy for unsuccessful ones.

MILLS BROTHERS CIRCUS

The Mills Brothers Circus was an Ohio-based show owned by brothers Jake, Jack and Harry Mills. All three men had previous experience in the circus business. In April 1940, the brothers pooled their money and bought out the Richard Brothers Circus. Their show debuted in Tallulah, Louisiana, and had its winter headquarters in Ashville, Ohio, for the first few years. The general operation was a mid-sized truck show that toured the Eastern Seaboard and Midwest states and enjoyed a favorable reputation with the public.

For decades, there were many small disreputable "grift shows" on the circus route. This, of course, gave the general industry a bad name and caused many potential customers to be skeptical of all circuses and especially sideshows. The Mills brothers pioneered partnering with local sponsors such as civic and fraternal organizations to sell tickets and promote the show before its arrival. This saved the need for an extensive in-house advance staff. The sponsoring organization shared an agreed portion of the ticket sales, and many planned their annual fundraising around the circus. Purchasing tickets from local organizations gave the public confidence in the credibility of the participating circus. Using local sponsorship proved to be extremely successful and was adopted as a goodwill promotional practice by other circuses.

Following the death of circus owner Paul M. Lewis, the Mills brothers purchased part of the Lewis Brothers Circus from Paul's widow and added the equipment to their circus inventory. A special behind-the-scene feature of

KISHMA GROTTO PRESENTS

MILLS Bros. CIRCUS
3 RING ★

SELECTED STARS
GLITTERING GIRLS
18 NATIONS

40 TONS OF ELEPHANTS

Twice daily 2 & 8 PM
DOORS OPEN 1 & 7 PM

RESERVED SEATS AND GENERAL ADM.
SEATS AT T. NEMETH SHOE REPAIR,
515 BRUSH ALLEY

UNDER ACRES OF CANVAS
Worlds Largest MOTORIZED
CIRCUS

The Mills Brothers Circus was another Ohio innovator. It pioneered using sponsors such as the Kiwanis or the Eagles aerie to sell tickets prior to the show coming to town. Circa 1943. *Dayton and Montgomery County Library.*

the Mills circus was a large, spotless cookhouse. Visitors in the show business were always invited to take part in sharing a meal. In addition to Ashville, Ohio, the circus also spent a few winters in Jefferson and Greenville, Ohio.

The Mills brothers were responsible for importing many circus acts and circus families into the United States, particularly after World War II. Many of the descendants of these families still perform in U.S. circuses today. In 1966, the circus was purchased by Sid Kellner, who started the James Brothers Circus. Jack Mills died on July 20, 1974.

TYPICAL CIRCUS SEASON ROUTE SCHEDULES AND CIRCUSES THAT WINTERED IN OHIO

Sells Brothers Enormous Shows, 1884

Eph Sells, Lewis Sells, Peter Sells, owners. Eph Sells, manager; Allen Sells, assistant manager; Peter Sells, general agent; James Stowe, equestrian director; James Morris, sideshow manager; W.N. Merrick, musical director. Winter quarters, Columbus, Ohio. Thirty-piece band. Fifty-cage menagerie. Show traveled 11,537 miles. December 9–10, returning to winter headquarters, 1,006 miles. December 11, arrived back in Columbus, Ohio.

*** November 17, San Marcos, Texas, Fritz, the big elephant, died here.

APRIL
16–19 – Columbus, Ohio
Sunday
21–23 – Cincinnati, Ohio
24 – Covington, Kentucky
25 – Paris, Kentucky
26 – Maysville, Kentucky
Sunday
28 – Richmond, Kentucky
29 – Winchester, Kentucky
30 – Lexington, Kentucky

MAY
1 – Frankfort, Kentucky
2–3 – Louisville, Kentucky
Sunday
5 – Rockport, Indiana
6 – Evansville, Indiana
7 – Vincennes, Indiana
8 – Terre Haute, Indiana
9–10 – Indianapolis, Indiana
Sunday
12 – Logansport, Indiana
13 – Lafayette, Indiana
14 – Crawfordsville, Indiana

15 – Danville, Illinois
16 – Champaign, Illinois
17 – Bloomington, Illinois
Sunday
19 – Peoria, Illinois
20 – Galesburg, Illinois
21 – Burlington, Iowa
22 – Quincy, Illinois
23 – Hannibal, Missouri
24 – Moberly, Missouri
Sunday
26 – Kansas City, Missouri
27 – Atchison, Missouri
28 – St. Joseph, Missouri
29 – Maryville, Missouri
30 – Bedford, Iowa
31 – Creston, Iowa

June
Sunday
2 – Des Moines, Iowa
3 – Newton, Iowa
4 – Iowa City, Iowa
5 – Cedar Rapids, Iowa
6 – Vinton, Iowa
7 – Waterloo, Iowa
Sunday
9–10 – Minneapolis, Minnesota
11 – St. Cloud, Minnesota
12 – Sauk Centre, Minnesota
13 – Alexandria, Minnesota
14 – Fergus Falls, Minnesota
Sunday
16 – Crookston, Minnesota
17 – Grand Forks, North Dakota
18 – Fargo, North Dakota
19 – Wahpeton, North Dakota
20 – Morris, Minnesota
21 – Litchfield, Minnesota

Sunday
23 – St. Paul, Minnesota
24 – Stillwater, Minnesota
25 – Hudson, Wisconsin
26 – Menominee, Wisconsin
27 – Eau Claire, Wisconsin
28 – Chippewa Falls, Wisconsin
30 – Stevens Point, Wisconsin

July
1 – Waupaca, Wisconsin
2 – Neenah, Wisconsin
3 – Oshkosh, Wisconsin
4 – Fond Du Lac, Wisconsin
5 – Green Bay, Wisconsin
Sunday
7 – Ishpeming, Michigan
8 – Negaunee, Michigan
9 – Escanaba, Michigan
10 – Florence, Michigan
11 – Memominee, Michigan
12 – Oconto, Wisconsin
Sunday
14 – Appleton, Wisconsin
15 – Wausau, Wisconsin
16 – New London, Wisconsin
17 – Manitowoc, Wisconsin
18 – Sheboygan, Wisconsin
19 – Milwaukee, Wisconsin
20 – Milwaukee, Wisconsin
21 – Watertown, Wisconsin
22 – Madison, Wisconsin
23 – Janesville, Wisconsin
24 – Elgin, Illinois
25 – Racine, Wisconsin
26 – Waukegan, Illinois
Sunday
28–31 – Chicago, Illinois
29 – Maryville, Missouri

30 – Bedford, Iowa
31 – Creston, Iowa

AUGUST
1–2 – Chicago, Illinois
Sunday
4 – Sterling, Illinois
5 – Sandwich, Illinois
6 – Princeton, Illinois
7 – Kewanee, Illinois
8 – Canton, Illinois
9 – Havana, Illinois
Sunday
11 – Petersburg, Illinois
12 – Carrollton, Illinois
13 – Alton, Illinois
14 – Louisiana, Missouri
15 – Fulton, Missouri
16 – Marshall, Missouri
Sunday
18 – Boonville, Missouri
19 – Sedalia, Missouri
20 – Clinton, Missouri
21 – Lexington, Missouri
22 – Warrensburg, Missouri
23 – Paola, Kansas
Sunday
25 – Ottawa, Kansas
26 – Harrisonville, Missouri
27 – Rich Hill, Missouri
28 – Carthage, Missouri
29 – Nevada, Missouri
30 – Ft. Scott, Kansas
Sunday

SEPTEMBER
1 – Parsons, Kansas
2 – Burlington, Kansas
3 – Emporia, Kansas

4 – Clay Center, Kansas
5 – Abilene, Kansas
6 – Minneapolis, Kansas
Sunday
8 – McPherson, Kansas
9 – Salina, Kansas
10 – Wamega, Kansas
11 – Topeka, Kansas
12 – Osage City, Kansas
13 – Marion Center, Kansas
15 – Eldorade, Kansas
16 – Newton, Kansas
17 – Hutchinson, Kansas
18 – Wichita, Kansas
19 – Wellington, Kansas
20 – Winfield, Kansas
Sunday
22 – Independence, Kansas
23 – Joplin, Missouri
24 – Neosha, Missouri
25 – Springfield, Missouri
26 – Pierce City, Missouri
27 – Fayetteville, Arkansas
Sunday
29 – Fort Smith, Arkansas
30 – Van Buren, Arkansas

OCTOBER
1 – Ozark, Arkansas
2 – Russellville, Arkansas
3 – Conway, Arkansas
4 – Little Rock, Arkansas
Sunday
6 – Malvern, Arkansas
7 – Hope, Arkansas
8 – Texarkana, Texas
9 – Clarksville, Texas
10 – Paris, Texas
11 – Bonham, Texas

Sunday
13 – Denison, Texas
14 – Sherman, Texas
15 – Gainesville, Texas
16 – Denton, Texas (one show only)
17 – Hillsboro, Texas
18 – Waco, Texas
Sunday
20 – Weatherford, Texas
21 – Fort Worth, Texas
22 – Henrietta, Texas
23 – Decatur, Texas
24 – Cleburne, Texas (one show only)
25 – Dallas, Texas
Sunday
27 – Belton, Texas
28 – Lampasas, Texas
29 – Caldwell, Texas
30 – Navasota, Texas
31 – Brenham, Texas

NOVEMBER
1 – Beeville, Texas
Sunday
3 – Galveston, Texas
4 – Houston, Texas
5 – Huntsville, Texas (one show)
6 – Crockett, Texas
7 – Longview, Texas

8 – Marshall, Texas
10 – Greenville, Texas
11 – Terrell, Texas
12 – Mineola, Texas
13 – Palestine, Texas
14 – Hearne, Texas (one show only)
15 – Austin, Texas
Sunday
17 – San Marcos, Texas ***
18 – San Antonio, Texas
19 – Gonzales, Texas
20 – Columbus, Texas
21 – La Grange, Texas
Sunday
24 – Beaumont, Texas
25 – Orange, Texas
26 – Lake Charles, Louisiana
27 – Vermillionville, Louisiana
28 – Morgan City, Louisiana
29 – Thibodauxville, Louisiana
30 – New Orleans, Louisiana
Sunday

DECEMBER
1–6 – New Orleans, Louisiana
7 – New Orleans, Louisiana
Sunday
8 – New Orleans, Louisiana
Season ends

Walter L. Main Circus Route, 1892

APRIL
23 – Geneva, Ohio
25 – Alliance, Ohio
26 – Salineville, Ohio
27 – Bellaire, Ohio
28 – Steubenville, Ohio

29 – Wellsburg, West Virginia
30 – Coshocton, Ohio

MAY
2 – New Lexington, Ohio
3 – Circleville, Ohio

4 – Lancaster, Ohio
5 – Logan, Ohio
6 – New Straitsville, Ohio
7 – Nelsonville, Ohio
9 – Athens, Ohio
10 – Point Pleasant, West Virginia
11 – Middleport, Ohio
12 – Corning, Ohio
13 – Marietta, Ohio
14 – Jackson, Ohio
16 – Greenfield, Ohio
17 – Wilmington, Ohio
18 – Xenia, Ohio
19 – Eaton, Ohio
20 – Greenville, Ohio
21 – Union City, Indiana
23 – Hartford City, Indiana
24 – Marion, Indiana
25 – Kokoma, Indiana [Kokomo]
26 – Martinsville, Indiana
27 – Spencer, Indiana
28 – Worthington, Indiana
30 – Brazil, Indiana
31 – Veedersburg, Indiana

JUNE
1 – Frankfort, Indiana
2 – Bluffton, Indiana
3 – Decatur, Indiana
4 – Rochester, Indiana
6 – Kankakee, Illinois
8 – Ottawa, Illinois
9 – Aurora, Illinois
10 – Belvidere, Illinois
11 – Kenosha, Wisconsin
13 – Watertown, Wisconsin
14 – Princeton, Wisconsin
15 – Sheboygan, Wisconsin
16 – Fond du Lac, Wisconsin

17 – De Pere, Wisconsin
18 – Appleton, Wisconsin
20 – Jefferson, Wisconsin
21 – Lodi, Wisconsin
22 – Reedsburg, Wisconsin
23 – Sparta, Wisconsin
24 – Elroy, Wisconsin
25 – Black River Falls, Wisconsin
29 – Rice Lake, Wisconsin
30 – Eau Claire, Wisconsin

JULY
1 – Wabash, Minnesota
2 – Lake City, Minnesota
4 – Necedah, Wisconsin
5 – Portage, Wisconsin
6 – Columbus, Wisconsin
7 – Oconomowoc, Wisconsin
8 – Elkhorn, Wisconsin
9 – Beloit, Wisconsin
11 – La Porte, Indiana
12 – Michigan City, Indiana
13 – Plymouth, Indiana
14 – Elwood, Indiana
15 – Muncie, Indiana
16 – New Castle, Indiana
18 – Cambridge City, Indiana
19 – Columbus, Indiana
20 – Seymour, Indiana
21 – Shoals, Indiana
22 – Washington, Indiana
23 – Vincennes, Indiana
26 – Fairfield, Illinois
27 – Flora, Illinois
28 – Salem, Illinois
29 – Carlyle, Illinois
30 – East St. Louis, Illinois

AUGUST

1 – Pacific, Missouri
2 – Steelville, Missouri
3 – Salem, Missouri
4 – Rolla, Missouri
5 – Lebanon, Missouri
6 – Marshfield, Missouri
8 – Bolivar, Missouri
9 – Aurora, Missouri
10 – Pierce City, Missouri
11 – Seneca, Missouri
12 – Galena, Kansas
13 – Webb City, Missouri
15 – Columbus, Kansas
16 – Oswego, Kansas
17 – Cherryvale, Kansas
18 – Freedonia, Kansas
19 – Eureka, Kansas
20 – Moline, Kansas
22 – Medicine Lodge, Kansas
23 – Harper, Kansas
25 – Independence, Kansas
26 – Iola, Kansas
27 – Garnet, Kansas
29 – Burlington, Kansas
30 – Lawrence, Kansas
31 – Burlingame, Kansas

SEPTEMBER

1 – Cottonwood Falls, Kansas
2 – Lyons, Kansas
3 – Ellsworth, Kansas
5 – Russell, Kansas
6 – Lincoln, Kansas
7 – Minneapolis, Kansas
9 – Marysville, Kansas
10 – Seneca, Kansas
12 – Hiawatha, Kansas
13 – Auburn, Nebraska

14 – Crete, Nebraska
15 – Seward, Nebraska
16 – Columbus, Nebraska
17 – Madison, Nebraska
19 – Albion, Nebraska
20 – Fullerton, Nebraska
21 – St. Paul, Nebraska
22 – Ord, Nebraska
23 – Ravenna, Nebraska
24 – Hastings, Nebraska
26 – McCook, Nebraska
27 – Arapahoe, Nebraska
28 – Alma, Nebraska
29 – Superior, Nebraska
30 – Washington, Kansas

OCTOBER

1 – Concordia, Kansas
3 – Atchison, Kansas
4 – Independence, Missouri
24 – Caldwell, Kansas
5 – Boonville, Missouri
6 – California, Missouri
7 – Warrensburg, Missouri
8 – Butler, Missouri
10 – Fort Scott, Kansas
11 – Pleasanton, Kansas
12 – Peola, Kansas
13 – Ottawa, Kansas
14 – Valley Falls, Kansas
15 – Junction City, Kansas
17 – Stockton, Kansas
18 – Osborn, Kansas
19 – Beloit, Kansas
20 – Abilene, Kansas
21 – Marion, Kansas
22 – McPherson, Kansas
24 – Pratt, Kansas
25 – Dodge City, Kansas

26 – Great Bend, Kansas

27 – Ness City, Kansas

28 – Larned, Kansas

29 – Stafford, Kansas

31 – Kingman, Kansas

NOVEMBER

1 – Wellington, Kansas

2 – Kingfisher, Oklahoma

3 – El Reno, Oklahoma Territory

4 – Oklahoma City, Oklahoma Territory

5 – Purcell, Indian Territory

7 – Guthrie, Oklahoma Territory

8 – Arkansas City, Kansas

9 – Sedan, Kansas

10 – Fort Gibson, Indian Territory

11 – Ozark, Arkansas

12 – Russellville, Arkansas

14 – Hot Springs, Arkansas

15 – Malvern, Arkansas

16 – Beebe, Arkansas

17 – Newport, Arkansas

18 – Batesville, Arkansas

19 – Paragould, Arkansas

The following is a list of circuses that wintered in Ohio during the 1900, 1906, 1908, 1910 and 1911 seasons. Some of the shows are not actual circuses, but traveling tented shows and street fairs.

Adell's Dog & Pony, Fort Recovery

Barber Brothers, Portsmouth

Forepaugh-Sells Brothers, Columbus

Mons La Place, Cambridge

Louis' Crescent, Trumbull

McCormick Brothers, Gallipolis

John Robinson Circus, Terrace Park and Cincinnati

Rhoda Royal, Geneva

Whitney Show, Attica

Happy Bob Robinson, Lancaster

Mons La Place, Lower Salem

Walter L. Main Circus, Geneva

Schaffer & Cook Bros., Portsmouth

Albert M. Wetter's, Massillon

Great American Water Circus, Ironton

Frank & Hermann's Vaudeville Show, Wapakoneta

Carl Hagenbeck Circus, Cincinnati

Gibb's Big Olympic Shows, Wapakoneta

Long Brothers Show, Circleville

Minnelli Bros., No. 1 & 2, Delaware

Stimmels' Society Circus, Springfield
Van Vranken Shows, Scott
Welsh Sisters' Show, Ohio City
William C. Heberling Circus, Fremont
Knight's 25-Cent Circus, Dunkirk
Long Brothers Show, Circleville
Joseph Lyar, Eaton
E.E. Eisenbarth, Marietta
S.F. Gorton's Circus, Toledo
Heber Brothers, Columbus
C.H. Knight, Dunkirk
Gus Lambrigger's, Orrville
E.G. Smith's Shows, Atwater

BIBLIOGRAPHY

"Annie Oakley Known by Gun; 'Champion Rifle Shot' a Sufficient Address – Chipped Ash from Wilhelm's Cigarette – Bullets Lifted Home Mortgage." *New York Times*, November 14, 1926. Retrieved March 26, 2018.

Apps, Jerry. *Ringlingville USA: The Stupendous Story of Seven Siblings and Their Stunning Circus Success*. Madison: Wisconsin Historical Society Press, 2005.

Bogdan, Robert. *Freak Show: Presenting Human Oddities for Amusement and Profit*. Chicago: University of Chicago Press. Reprint edition 1990.

Bradbury, Joseph T. "Circus Wagon History File." *Bandwagon* (March–April 1958): 5–6.

Carlyon, David. *Dan Rice: The Most Famous Man You've Never Heard Of*. New York: Public Affairs–Perseus Books Group, 2001.

Conley, Henry. "The Auction of the Forepaugh & Sells Bros. Circus." *Bandwagon* (April 1943): 6–7.

Conover, Richard E. *"Give'em A John Robinson Circus; A documentary on the Old John Robinson Circus,"* Xenia, OH: Self-published, 1965.

———. *The Great Forepaugh Show: America's Largest Circus from 1864 to 1894.* Xenia, OH: Self-published, 1959.

———. "The Origin of the John Robinson Circus and the Myth of 1824," *Bandwagon* (June 1953).

Cooke, Louis. "Walter L. Main." *Bandwagon* (May–June 1967): 3–13.

Covert, Ralph. *Sawdust and Spangles: The Amazing Life of W.C. Coup*. New York: Abrams Books, 2007.

Culhane, John. *The American Circus, An Illustrated History*. New York: Henry Holt and Company, 1990.

Dahlinger, Frederick, Jr. "The Bode Wagon Company." *Bandwagon* (November–December 1982): 5–11.

Duble, Charlie. "Era of Robinson Shows and Pageantry on Main Street." *Hobby Bandwagon* (January–February 1950): 6.

Eckley, Wilton. *The American Circus*. Boston: Twayne Publishers, 1984.

Green, Shorty. *Route Book for Sells Brothers Circus and S.H. Barrett Circus 1889*.

Gusler, Howard A. "John Robinson Quarters." *Bandwagon* (October 1953): 3.

Hartzman, Marc. *American Sideshow: An Encyclopedia of History's Most Wondrous and Curiously Strange Performers*. New York: Jeremy P. Tarcher/Penguin, 2005.

Heber, Robert A. *Heber Brothers Greater Show: My Great Grandfather Had a Circus*. Publisher, Columbus, OH: R.A. Heber, 2001.

Hoh, LaVahn G., and William H. Rough. *Step Right Up! The Adventure of Circus in America*. White Hall, VA: Betterway Publications, Inc., 1990.

"John Robinson Circus Parade 1893." *Bandwagon* (September–October 1957): 9.

Kasper, Shirl. *Annie Oakley*. Norman: University of Oklahoma Press, 1992.

Keating, W.L. *Route Book for Sells Brothers Circus 1878*.

King, Orin C. *The Circus World of Willie Sells*. Topeka, KS: Shawnee County Historical Society, 1983

Kotar, S.L. *The Rise of the American Circus, 1716–1899*. Jefferson, NC: McFarland & Company, 2011.

Krohn, Katherine E. *Wild West Women*. Minneapolis, MN: Lerner Publications, 2005.

Long, Fred E. "The Great Circus Train Wreck of 1893." *Pennsylvania Heritage* (Fall 1984).

Madden, Charles *Route Book for Sells Brothers Circus 1886*.

McKennon, Joe. *Horse Dun Trail: Saga of the American Circus*. Sarasota, FL: Carnival Publishers, 1975.

McOwen, W.A., and Gus Stevens. *Route Book for Sells Brothers Circus 1882*. Jacksonville, FL: Ashmead Bros. Printers & Binders.

Ogden, Tom. *Two Hundred Years of the American Circus: From Aba-Daba to the Zoppe-Zavatta Troupe*. New York: Facts on File, 1993.

Olsen, Melvin J. "Newspaper Story Places John Robinson on Raymond & Wahring Show of 1839." *Bandwagon* (April–May 1954): 3–4.

Parker, Joe O. "The Great Jacksonville Circus Fight." *Bandwagon* (January–February 2006): 18–21.

Parkinson, Bob. *"The John Robinson Circus,"* *Bandwagon* (March–April 1962).

Patzer, Nancy. "Circus Town! Sells Brothers Called Columbus Home." *Short North Gazette*, 1999.

Pfening, Fred D., Jr. "The Great Fred J. Mack Circus." *Bandwagon* (June 1955): 5.

———. "Sells Brothers." *Bandwagon* (January–February 1964): 4–13.

———. "So You Always Wanted to Own a Circus." *Bandwagon* (July–August 1984): 4–12.

Riley, Glenda. *The Life and Legacy of Annie Oakley.* Norman: University of Oklahoma Press, 1994.

Sabia, Robert. *Route Book for Walter L. Main Circus 1898.*

Sells, Tim. *When Dublin Wasn't Doublin'.* Self-published, 2012.

Simon, Linda. *The Greatest Shows on Earth: A History of the Circus.* London: Reaktion Books, Ltd., 2014.

Slout, William L. *Ink from a Circus Press Agent: An Anthology of Circus History from the Pen of Charles Day.* San Bernardino, CA: Borgo Press, 1995.

———. *Olympians of the Sawdust Circle: A Biographical Dictionary of the Nineteenth Century American Circus.* Rockville, MD: Wildside Press LLC; Paperback, 2009.

Speaight, George. *A History of the Circus.* San Diego: A.S. Barnes and Company, 1980.

St. Leon, Mark. *Spangles & Sawdust: The Circus in Australia.* Richmond, Victoria, Australia: Greenhouse Publications, 1983.

Taber, Bob. "Robinson's Three-Ring Circus of 1910." Bob Taber Press Sheet. *Bandwagon* (Christmas 1955): 5.

Taylor, William A. *Centennial History of Columbus & Franklin County.* Columbus, OH: S.J. Clarke Publishing Co., 1909, pp. 558–562.

Thayer, Stuart. *Annals of the American Circus 1793–1860.* Seattle: Dauven & Thayer, 1992.

Washington, Harriet A. *Medical Apartheid: The Dark History of Medical Experimentation on Black Americans from Colonial Times to the Present.* New York: Anchor Books. Reprint paperback edition 2008.

Weber, Susan. *The American Circus.* New Haven, CT: Yale University Press, 2012.

Weisheimer, Carl. *Sellsville, Circa 1900.* 1971.

Library Resources

Ashtabula County District Library; Brooklyn (New York) Public Library; Chillicothe and Ross County Public Library; University of Cincinnati Library Archive; Cincinnati & Hamilton County Library; Cleveland Public Library; Columbus Metropolitan Library; Library of Congress; Dayton Public Library; Illinois State University Library; Indianapolis Public Library Archive; Kansas City, Kansas Public Library; Kansas Historical Society; University of Kentucky Library Archive; Marietta–Washington County Public Library; Ohio History Connection; State Library of Ohio; Peru Indiana Public Library; Tyrone-Snyder Public Library.

Newspapers

Altoona (PA) Tribune
Arkansas State Gazette & Democrat
Ashtabula (OH) Weekly Telegraph
Bellefontaine (OH) Republican
Belvidere (IL) Daily Republican
Brooklyn (NY) Eagle
Cairo (IL) Bulletin
Cedar Rapids (IA) Times
Chicago InterOcean
Cincinnati Chronicle
Cincinnati Inquirer
Circus Bulletin
Cleveland (OH) Herald
Columbus Daily Times
Columbus Dispatch
Columbus Record
Coshocton Morning Tribune
Daily Press (Willington, KS)
Davenport (IA) Gazette
Decatur (IL) Daily Review
Delaware (OH) Gazette
Detroit Free Press
Evansville (IN) Daily Journal
Greenville (OH) Journal
Holmes Co. Republican (Millersburg, OH)

Indiana (PA) Progress
Iola (KS) Register
Lansing (MI) State Journal
Lebanon (OH) Patriot
Lima (OH) Daily News
Mansfield (OH) Herald
Mansfield (OH) Weekly Shield & Banner
Medina County (OH) Gazette
Memphis Daily Appeal
News-Herald (Hillsboro, OH)
Noble County Leader
Ohio State Journal
Owensboro (KY) Messenger
Paducah (KY) Sun
Portsmouth (OH) Enquirer
Salem (OH) Daily News
Stark County (OH) Democrat
Summit County (OH) Beacon
Toledo (OH) Blade
Toledo (OH) Times
Tyrone (PA) Daily Herald
Van Wert (OH) Times
Warren (PA) Ledger
Wilmington (OH) Journal
Xenia (OH) Sentinel

ABOUT THE AUTHOR

Conrade Hinds is originally from Nashville, Tennessee, and a graduate of Ball State University in Muncie, Indiana, where he studied architecture and industrial technology. He has lived in Central Ohio for forty years and previously worked for the Franklin County Engineer's Office and several architecture firms. He is a registered architect and a retired projects manager with the City of Columbus Department of Public Utilities. He is also a retired adjunct faculty member in the Engineering Technology Department at Columbus State Community College.

As an author, he enjoys researching and writing about forgotten history. He has written two other published books. The first, titled *The Great Columbus Experiment of 1908*, is about the major role the City of Columbus played in developing state-of-the-art water and wastewater infrastructure that once placed in service would quickly eradicate a typhoid epidemic. The second, titled *Columbus and the Great Flood of 1913*, chronicles the events leading up to a record-breaking devastating flood and the aftermath that left the industrial Midwest of America severely crippled prior to World War I.

As a licensed auctioneer, he likes to give back to the community by donating his services to a variety of charitable fundraising events. Conrade and his wife, Janet, have four adult children and four grandchildren and enjoy attending rural country festivals and visiting historic sites in America and Europe. He is also a storyteller and incorporates forgotten history and the use of puppets and marionettes in his presentations.